# JEWELRY

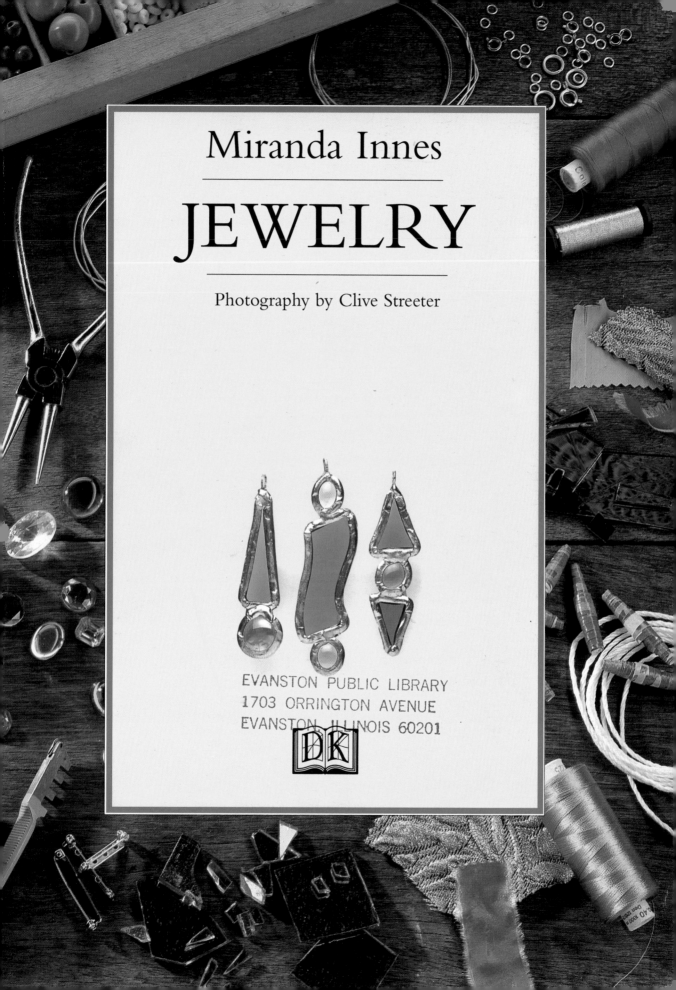

# Miranda Innes

---

# JEWELRY

---

### Photography by Clive Streeter

DK

A DK PUBLISHING BOOK

Created and produced by
COLLINS & BROWN LIMITED
London House
Great Eastern Wharf
Parkgate Road
London SW11 4NQ

| | |
|---|---|
| **Project Editor** | Heather Dewhurst |
| **Managing Editor** | Sarah Hoggett |
| **Editorial Assistant** | Corinne Asghar |
| | |
| **Art Director** | Roger Bristow |
| **Art Editor** | Marnie Searchwell |
| | |
| **Photography** | Clive Streeter |
| **Stylist** | Ali Edney |

First American edition, 1996
2 4 6 8 10 9 7 5 3 1
Published in the United States by DK Publishing, Inc.
95 Madison Avenue, New York, NY 10016

A catalog record is available from the Library of Congress.
ISBN 0-7894-0433-8

Reproduced in Singapore by Daylight Colour Art
Printed and bound in France by Pollina - n° 68961 - B

# Contents

## Paper and Fabric Jewelry

## Bead and Glass Jewelry

## Wood and Metal Jewelry

# Introduction

JEWELRY CAN BE DIVIDED into two categories: the kind that needs an armed guard, and the kind that has no other purpose than to give you a frisson of pleasure. This is not the book for people who feel naked without a sheik's ransom of diamonds from head to toe; it is for anyone who wants to look like a million dollars for the price of a daily newspaper. Within its pages, you will learn how to make perfectly respectable-looking necklaces and earrings, beads, bangles, and brooches, along with a few forays into the wilder interpretations of jewelry, and one or two bold examples of delightful kitsch. The complete spectrum of brilliant and glittering bijoux, baubles, and geegaws is covered. Jewelry should be fun, as well as decorative, and making it yourself doubles your sense of satisfaction.

None of the projects in this book costs as much as a minuscule pair of gold ear-studs,

**Rainbow Colors**
*Brightly painted stripes, spots, and squiggles adorn a wooden brooch.*

most do not need expensive equipment, and a few hours is enough time to make any of them. Some of the designs are more classic than others, you may find that your children will covet some of the pieces, and one or two are obviously contemporary fashion items; however, all of the techniques shown can easily be adapted to suit whatever is the current essential accessory.

Many of the techniques shown in the book may remind you of your childhood. Rolled paper beads are such an example; while no one could call them sophisticated, they are fun to make and great to wear on vacation. Papier-mâché is another kindergarten pastime that resurfaces here in the more glamorous guise of jewelry making, and it may evoke fond reminiscences as you pulp your paper and transform it with paint and gilding. Vanishing muslin is a more recent and technological discovery; lacy, cobweb-fine pieces can be made simply using colorful

**Painted Tin**
*These welded tin brooches are painted with glossy enamel paints.*

**Harlequin Scraps**
*Bright snippets and scraps of fabric create a brilliant patchwork bangle in jester's motley.*

embroidery thread and a sewing machine, following a technique that results in a cross between satin and lace, embellished with tiny beads or sequins as you wish. Felt is another fabric with potential; it is the oldest man-made textile and was all the rage in the better class of cave, but there is nothing primitive about the brilliant baubles we show you how to make.

**Newsy Necklace**
*The printed word provides the decoration in this inventive papier-mâché necklace.*

A close perusal of the gallery sections will fill you with further ideas, building on those you may already have dreamed up.

**Bright Baubles**
*Predyed woolen fleece and shiny studs combine in an original pair of earrings.*

Using thin wire instead of thread for beading, for example, gives a rigid structure that might be exactly what you need to make an unassuming yet stylish crown for occasions when a touch of the regal is required. In fact, once you get the hang of using wire, you could find yourself turning out chokers and chandeliers. Mosaic techniques also adapt to all kinds of objects, and mosaics can be built up using resin, or on a more durable base of metal or wood if you decide to make a glittering picture frame.

This book gives you the basic recipes, for which you can invent variations to your heart's content. You will soon begin to see shining possibilities in the most unexpected places. The seashore will become a treasure trove, with new glories thrown up by every passing tide. Mundane trips to the lumberyard and hardware and building-supply stores will induce an overwhelming state of trance as you size up the possibilities of that copper wire, or those wing-nuts. Notions counters in sewing stores will have you mesmerized with their rainbow stacks of silks, glossy threads, sequins, beads, and buttons. You might even find yourself exploring the musty corners of thrift stores in search of abandoned necklaces and broken bracelets to recycle into dazzling and original brooches and hat pins. As you begin to extend your tool kit and add such invaluable items as tin snips, superglue, round-nosed pliers, and earring findings, you will start to notice the clever little touches that complete a piece of jewelry and give it a professional air. This book will start you off making jewelry, and give you ideas enough to keep you sparkling throughout many party seasons.

**Light Show**
*Colored glass and bright droplets add a glowing luminosity to jewelry.*

# Basic Materials

YOU CAN MAKE stunning jewelry with very little outlay using the most basic of materials. With only colored paper and paint, you can make papier-mâché or rolled paper bead necklaces, interspersing with wooden or glass beads. Alternatively, you can collect remnants of fabric, and stitch soft padded earrings and brooches, and embellish these with beads and embroidery. If you have a toolbox handy, you could tackle thin wood, sheet copper, steel, or brass to create and decorate jewelry. Colored sheet glass is another wonderful material you can use, either shaped with a glass cutter for

Fancy beads

**◄ Glass and Beads**
*Colored or mirror glass is excellent for mosaic pieces, and it is easily cut to the desired shape with a glass cutter. Beads come in every color and material. Simply thread them onto waxed polyester thread or wire to make jewelry.*

Colored and mirror glass

Wooden beads

Pressed leaves

**▼ Paper and Cardboard**
*Use colored and plain paper, even newspaper, to make and decorate your jewelry. Cardboard makes an ideal base for papier-mâché brooches and earrings.*

Glass nuggets

Seed beads

Raffia

Waxed thread

Assorted papers and cardboard

**◄ Threading Materials**
*Use waxed thread or nylon-coated miniature wire cable to thread strands of lightweight or tiny seed beads and make necklaces and bangles. Raffia is an ideal material for larger, heavier beads, and it offers a rich texture and natural, earthy appearance.*

Miniature wire cable

mosaic jewelry or wrapped with channeled lead for stained glass pieces. Decorate your jewelry with paints, inks, silk, threads, pressed leaves, notions, or even hardware. The one essential material you need for threading beads is waxed thread or miniature wire cable; alternatively, you could use raffia.

## ▼ Fabrics

*Burlap is the base for hand-hooked jewelry; vanishing muslin is used in machine embroidery. You can make all kinds of sumptuous baubles from pieces of silk and fabric scraps, or bright, chunky felt beads from predyed woolen fleece.*

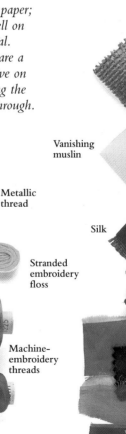

Burlap

## ◄ Paints and Inks

*Paper jewelry can be quickly transformed with a coat of paint. Gouache is best for paper; acrylics work well on wood and metal. Colored inks are a good alternative on wood, allowing the grain to show through.*

Acrylic and gouache paints

Water-based ink

Vanishing muslin

Silk

## ► Threads

*You have the whole spectrum of color and texture at your disposal when you use threads to embellish your jewelry, ranging from glistening metallic threads to silky, stranded embroidery floss.*

Metallic thread

Stranded embroidery floss

## ▼ Metals and Wood

*Sheet metal and thin wood are easy to work with, provided you have the right tools. Channeled lead is perfect for wrapping around pieces of glass, while metal tubing can be used to make decorative rivets.*

Machine-embroidery threads

Fabric scraps

Sheet copper, steel, and brass

Thin balsa wood

Silver tubing

Channeled lead

Sanded sheet steel

Predyed fleece

# Fastenings and Tools

ONCE YOU HAVE MADE the decorative part of your jewelry, you will need to attach a fastening to it, to enable you to wear it. There is a wide variety of findings, pins, rings, hooks, and wires readily available for you to choose from. Depending on the type of jewelry you are making, you will also need various tools to shape, cut, and polish your pieces. With a bit of ingenuity, you can make do with what you have at home, then gradually collect more items as and when you need them.

### ▶ Fastenings

*There are all kinds of fastenings available, in a huge variety of shapes and styles. You can use them alone, to complete your jewelry, or in conjunction with each other, to link elements together. Use findings or bolt and split rings for necklaces, hooks for earrings, and pin backs for brooches. Bell caps are useful for neatening ragged ends.*

Earring findings

Split rings

Pin backs

Necklace findings

Bell cap fastenings

Bolt rings

Hat pins

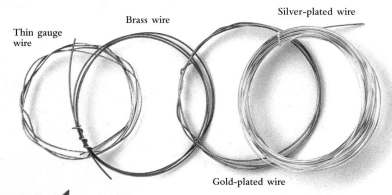

Thin gauge wire

Brass wire

Silver-plated wire

Gold-plated wire

### ◀ Wires

*Wire is essential in jewelry-making, and it can have several purposes. You can loop wire with pliers to hook elements of a necklace or bracelet together, or thread beads onto wire to add another section to earrings. You can also make decorative coils to add to earrings, necklaces, or hat pins.*

Hook

### ◀ Sewing Tools

*Pins and needles are vital for making fabric jewelry. A fine beading needle is perfect for sewing tiny beads onto fabric. For embroidery, stretch the fabric in a hoop. A hook is needed to pull loops of fabric through coarse burlap.*

Embroidery hoop

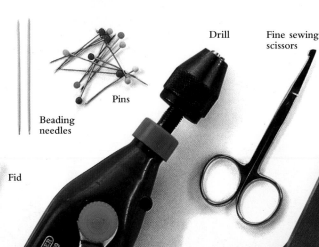

Beading needles

Pins

Fid

Drill

Fine sewing scissors

Sewing scissors

## ▶ Skewers and Toothpicks

*Toothpicks are very useful for positioning tiny pieces of decoration; wooden skewers can hold beads while they are drying; and knitting needles are good for wrapping paper around to make rolled beads.*

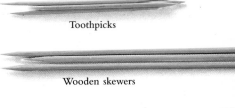

Toothpicks

Wooden skewers

Knitting needles

## ▼ Solder and Flux

*There are different types of solder and flux, but they all fuse metal to metal. Apply the flux to the surface of the metal, then, holding both pieces of metal together, melt the solder on top to fuse them.*

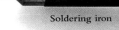

Soldering iron

Solder

Metal files

Flux

## ▶ Punching Tools

*You can create wonderful textured patterns on metal using a hammer and tin punch. Place the metal on an anvil, hold a tin punch vertically on the metal, and hammer it sharply. Repeat to create a surface pitted with dots.*

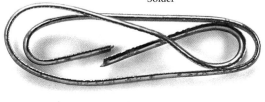

Hammer and tin punch

## ▼ Cutting and Shaping Tools

*Sewing scissors are essential for cutting large areas of fabric; smaller scissors are useful for detailed work. A craft knife is good for cutting paper and cardboard. You need a glass cutter for cutting glass for mosaic jewelry. To cut wood or metal, use a coping saw — you may need a drill to make holes before sawing. Tin snips can also be used to cut metal. Use metal files to smooth the cut edges. Pliers are useful for bending and shaping wire into loops and hooks. A fid is used to press channeled lead securely onto the edge of a piece of glass.*

Pumice powder

Miniature anvil

## ▶ Polishing Tools

*Use pumice powder on a brass brush moistened with water to burnish sheet metals. Give your jewelry a final shine with a glass brush before polishing with a soft cloth.*

Brass brush and glass brush

Metal ruler

Craft knife

Coping saw

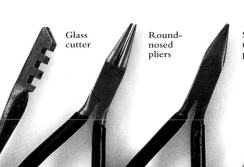

Glass cutter

Round-nosed pliers

Square-nosed pliers

Tin snips

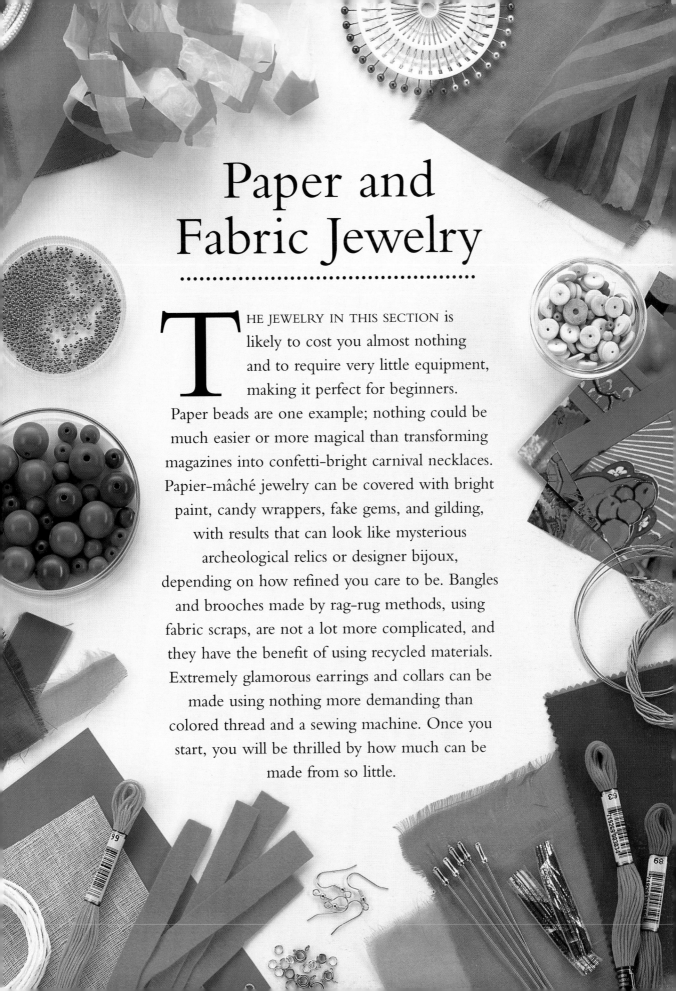

# Paper and Fabric Jewelry

THE JEWELRY IN THIS SECTION is likely to cost you almost nothing and to require very little equipment, making it perfect for beginners. Paper beads are one example; nothing could be much easier or more magical than transforming magazines into confetti-bright carnival necklaces. Papier-mâché jewelry can be covered with bright paint, candy wrappers, fake gems, and gilding, with results that can look like mysterious archeological relics or designer bijoux, depending on how refined you care to be. Bangles and brooches made by rag-rug methods, using fabric scraps, are not a lot more complicated, and they have the benefit of using recycled materials. Extremely glamorous earrings and collars can be made using nothing more demanding than colored thread and a sewing machine. Once you start, you will be thrilled by how much can be made from so little.

# Paper Rainbows

**MATERIALS**
Sheets of
colored paper
Polyvinyl white glue
Wooden beads
Waxed thread

**EQUIPMENT**
Ruler
Pen
Scissors
Artist's brush
Fine knitting needle
Wooden skewers
Dish

**A**S ADORNMENT GOES, there are few things simpler than rolled paper beads. Any child can make them, and any adult with a sense of drama could wear them with panache. Beloved of our great-grandmothers, paper beads utilize the most basic commodities that most people have on hand – bright paper and glue. From these humble beginnings, splendid results follow.

Magazines can yield polychrome pages for free, but if you take a look in any store selling wrapping paper, you will see an Aladdin's cave of brilliant possibilities. There are handmade papers in subtle hues and refined textures, bright, smooth construction paper, paper inlaid with glittering confetti in gold and silver, and paper patterned with colorful marbled, mottled, metallic, and speckled designs.

If your jewels cost nothing, you can afford to be generous; rolled paper beads look good in quantity. Vary the shape of your beads by cutting differently shaped paper triangles, and dip them in tinted varnish instead of colorless white glue. You can't go wrong with paper; you can make anything from huge, rough beads to tiny, shiny ones. There is every excuse to experiment and enjoy yourself.

**Festival Necklace**
*As joyful and theatrical as Mardi Gras, this kaleidoscopic collar is carnival and Christmas rolled into one.*

**Party Colors**
*By choosing different spacers and colored papers, combining many strands or just one, and varying the size of the beads, you can create dozens of easy variations on this jaunty theme.*

## Making the Beads
*You do not need great artistic skill to make paper beads;
even children can make them. All you need are magazines,
scissors, a dab of glue, and a knitting needle.*

Colorful
magazine pages

Waxed thread

Polyvinyl
white glue

Wooden beads
and spacers

**1** *Search through magazines for colorful pages and cut them out. Sort the pages into related colors. Taking one sheet at a time, divide it into triangles. To do this, mark every 2in (5cm) along one edge. Repeat on the opposite edge of the paper, but this time starting 1in (2.5cm) in from the side. Using a ruler and pen, join the marks on opposite sides of the paper to make long, narrow triangles.*

**2** *Cut out the triangles with a pair of sharp scissors. Each triangle will make one bead. To make a necklace about 30in (75cm) long, you will need approximately 24 beads.*

**3** *Determine which side of the paper is the most colorful. Turn the triangles over and brush glue on the reverse side, starting about 1¼in (3cm) from the base and gluing to the tip. Glue three triangles at a time, before proceeding to the next step.*

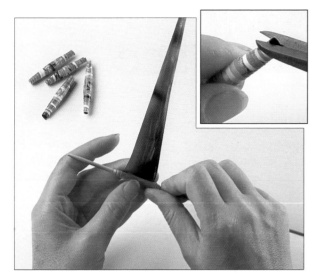

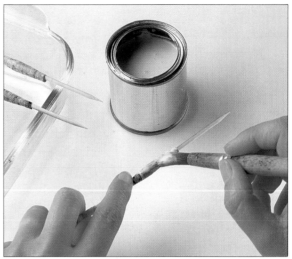

**4** *Wrap the unglued end of a paper triangle around a knitting needle. Roll up the paper tightly around the needle. When you reach the tip, pull the knitting needle out and snip off any untidy ends with scissors (see inset). Repeat with each triangle, and let the rolled beads dry.*

**5** *When the beads are dry, thread three at a time on a wooden skewer, spacing them apart. Using an artist's brush, paint each bead all over with a coat of glue, which acts as a varnish. Prop the skewers over a bowl, and let the beads dry for an hour.*

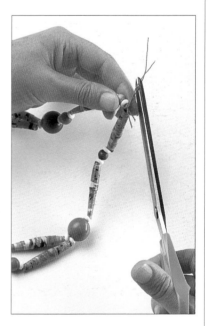

**6** *Choose wooden beads to complement the paper beads. String one strand of beads on waxed thread, alternating paper beads with wooden beads. Repeat to thread a second, shorter strand. These strands will be joined together to make one necklace, so choose beads carefully. Leave 8in (20cm) of thread free at each end for knotting.*

**7** *Join the two strands of beads together at each end by threading both strands through one wooden bead on each end. Then thread three or four more rolled paper beads on to the doubled strands at each end of the necklace.*

**8** *Knot the four threads together securely. Trim the ends of the thread with scissors, then paint the knot with glue for extra security. Push the knot inside a paper bead so it is not visible, and move all the beads around the thread accordingly.*

# Pebble Necklace

## MATERIALS

Nylon cord
Matte adhesive tape
Nylon thread
Raffia
Assorted pebble beads
Natural linen thread
2 bell cap fastenings
Split ring
Polyvinyl white glue
Bolt ring

## EQUIPMENT

Scissors
Tape measure
Needle
Large-eyed needle
Toothpick

THIS BEACHCOMBER'S COLLECTION of pebbles and raffia is put together with casual grace, making it the perfect necklace for summer. If you are adept with power tools, you could make a wearable souvenir of lazy summer days using actual pebbles or shells collected along the shoreline instead of beads. Drill a hole in the pebbles using a fine masonry drill bit, then thread them together with fine linen thread or gardening twine.

Making this necklace involves the technique of wrapping; here, raffia and linen thread are used to give an earthy, natural look, but you could also try using colored linen or embroidery floss allied with glass droplets and metal beads, to produce something rich and festive. Once you feel confident with wrapping, you can use it for lustrous braided cords, with which you can make chokers, or even belts if ambition grips you. What distinguishes this necklace from the one that a child might make is the attention to details; the linen spiral is applied very evenly over the raffia, and the neat closure with metal bell caps makes a huge difference.

**Seashore Chic**
*Easy to make and easy to wear, this necklace will be your favorite summer accessory. When the nights close in and the seasons change, you will be cheeringly reminded of hot sun and the sound of the waves every time you see it.*

**Desert Detritus**
*Terra-cotta and bone are perfectly juxtaposed in this talismanic necklace. Such classy flotsam could be interspersed equally effectively with frosted and stone-washed glass or buttons.*

## Assembling the Necklace
*The elements of this necklace — the pebble beads, raffia,*
*and linen thread — make you think of summer.*

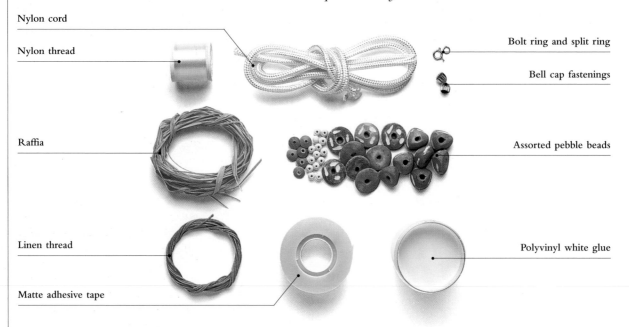

Nylon cord

Nylon thread

Raffia

Linen thread

Matte adhesive tape

Bolt ring and split ring

Bell cap fastenings

Assorted pebble beads

Polyvinyl white glue

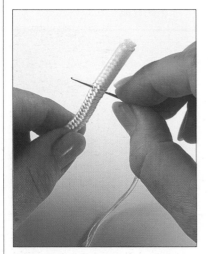

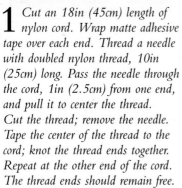

**1** Cut an 18in (45cm) length of nylon cord. Wrap matte adhesive tape over each end. Thread a needle with doubled nylon thread, 10in (25cm) long. Pass the needle through the cord, 1in (2.5cm) from one end, and pull it to center the thread. Cut the thread; remove the needle. Tape the center of the thread to the cord; knot the thread ends together. Repeat at the other end of the cord. The thread ends should remain free.

**2** Taking a length of raffia, lay the end of it along one end of the cord. Begin to wrap the raffia around the cord, covering and securing the end of the raffia as you go. Wrap evenly, leaving no visible gaps. When you reach the end of a length of raffia, place the end against the first 2in (5cm) of the new length, and wrap over the top to conceal the ends. Continue wrapping in this way until the entire cord is covered.

**3** To secure the raffia at the end of the cord, thread a large-eyed needle with the raffia and push the needle back between the cord and its wrapping for about 1in (2.5cm). Bring the needle out, and cut the raffia close to the wrapping.

**4** *Make a beaded section to hang from the wrapped cord. Fold a length of raffia in half. Thread the looped end through a flat-disk pebble bead, pass the two raffia ends through the loop, and tighten. Thread several pebble beads on to the doubled raffia, then split the raffia and thread a bead on to each strand. Knot each strand.*

**5** *Knot the two strands together. Pass the raffia strands one at a time through the center of a flat-disk bead, one from the front and one from the back of the bead, so the strands cross in the hole. Knot the strands together directly above the disk, then thread on another bead and knot the raffia to complete the section.*

**6** *Tie the beaded section securely to the center of the wrapped cord. Using a large-eyed needle, thread the raffia ends through the wrapping on each side of the knot, and cut close to the wrapped cord. Attach more beaded sections to the cord on each side of the central hanging beaded section, as above.*

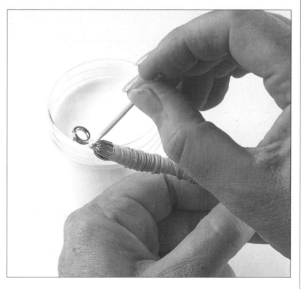

**7** *Starting about ¾in (2cm) in from one end of the cord, lay linen thread against the raffia-covered cord and wrap it around the cord, as before. After approximately ¾in (2cm) of wrapping, make a long diagonal wrap so about ⅝in (1.5cm) of raffia is left showing, before wrapping another section of ¾in (2cm). Continue like this until you reach the hanging beaded section, then wrap more densely here and leave the knots as a feature. Wrap until you reach the end of the cord. Finish off as in step 3.*

**8** *Thread the four strands of nylon thread at one end of the necklace through a bell cap fastening; slide the bell cap down to cover the end of the cord. Thread a split ring on to two of the strands of nylon, then knot all four strands to secure. Cut the ends and, using a toothpick, dab with glue to seal. Thread a bell cap on to the other end of the cord, as before. Thread two of the four strands of nylon through the end loop of a bolt ring, knot securely, cut the ends, and seal with glue. Let dry.*

# Star-Spangled Stunner

**MATERIALS**

Cardboard
Burlap
Fabric strips, ½in (12mm) wide
Foil strips, ½in (12mm) wide
Latex adhesive
Clear adhesive
Black felt
Black sewing thread
Pin back
Superglue

**EQUIPMENT**

Scissors
Marker pen
Embroidery hoop
Hook
Needle

EVERYONE KNOWS that recycling is worthy, but some people have discovered the secret of making it fun. An inauspicious trio of thrift-store fabric, burlap, and old potato chip bags has been transformed into this star brooch of stylish, insouciant braggadocio, which has the great added advantage of being shamelessly showy, yet unlikely to attract muggers or to need stowing away in the safe.

If you have never experienced the immense smug pleasure of making something from nothing, this is your chance. This brooch is a miniature version of the rag rugs with which our grandparents used to cheat poverty and icy winter drafts. You could use any materials; bright felt, wool, old T-shirts, shiny satin, or Thai silk would all have a particular and attractive quality. Here, the dark fabric is in witty contrast to the plastic foil, which produces a texture and steely glint reminiscent of chain mail. In the bad old days, it took an entire winter to make a hearth rug. This handsome star could grace your lapel in a matter of hours; if you prefer, you could make a hooked heart or daisy, or even a Christmas tree.

**Star Attraction**
*This star brooch does not belong to the discreet category of jewelry; it is designed to be worn with a smile and to be greeted with a giggle.*

**Loop Story**
*If old potato chip bags and strips of fabric can be said to dance, these brooches have a definite funky rhythm. For extra sparkle, you could sew on a sprinkling of sequins.*

## Hooking the Star

*Achieving even loops will become easy with a little practice, and you can raid your scrap bag for appealing colors and textures of fabric.*

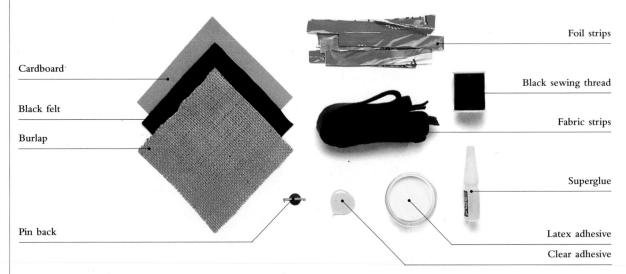

Cardboard

Black felt

Burlap

Pin back

Foil strips

Black sewing thread

Fabric strips

Superglue

Latex adhesive

Clear adhesive

1 *Make a cardboard template of the shape of your brooch. This brooch design is a star, but you could choose any shape you like. Using a marker, draw around this shape on to a piece of burlap, leaving a border of at least 3in (7.5cm) around your design.*

2 *Put the burlap in an embroidery hoop so the design lies centrally in the hoop. Begin hooking fabric strips around the outline of the star. Hold the fabric strip beneath the burlap with one hand, then push the hook through the burlap from above with the other hand. Guide the fabric strip over the hook to create a loop (see inset). Pull the hook back through the burlap, bringing the end of the fabric strip to the top side.*

3 *Push the hook back through the burlap just next to the strip, guide the fabric on to the hook, and pull it through the burlap to the top side, creating a loop on the surface of the burlap. Pull the fabric strip back gently until the loop is at the required height. Continue forming a line of loops in this way around the star. At the end of a fabric strip, bring the end through to the top side of the burlap and trim to the height of the loops.*

**4** *After you have completed an outline around the star shape, begin to hook foil strips in the center of the star, working from the center outward until you have filled the design. Make sure the foil loops are an even height.*

**5** *Remove the burlap from the hoop and lay it face-down on a flat surface. Cut the excess burlap away to leave a border of 1in (2.5cm) around the star shape. Using a piece of cardboard, smear a thin layer of latex adhesive over the back of the star shape and on to the border.*

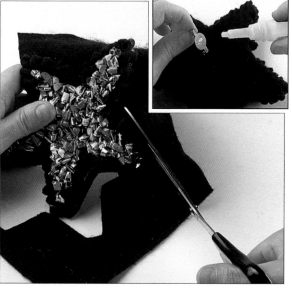

**6** *Using scissors, make diagonal cuts into the burlap border of the star shape, right up to the hooked area. Fold the burlap in toward the center of the star shape, squeezing it together so that it sticks down. Trim off any excess burlap. Let the star shape dry for 10 minutes until the glue becomes clear.*

**7** *Apply a thin layer of clear adhesive on the back of the star. Stick a piece of black felt over the glue. Trim away the excess felt around the edge of the star shape. Using a needle and black thread, slipstitch the felt to the edge of the star to secure the felt even more and neaten the brooch. Attach a pin back to the center back of the brooch using Superglue (see inset). Let the glue dry for an hour before wearing the brooch.*

# Patchwork Bangle

## MATERIALS

Scraps of brightly colored fabric

Strip of muslin, 12 x 2in (30 x 5cm)

Colored cotton thread

2 strips of plain fabric, 12 x 1in (30 x 2.5cm)

String

Batting

Sewing thread

Contrasting fabric, cut on the bias, 12 x 3in (30 x 7.5cm)

Stranded embroidery floss

## EQUIPMENT

Scissors

Pins

Sewing machine and darning foot

Needle

RAID YOUR SCRAP BAG for tiny snippets and scraps of fabric, and stitch a rainbow with brightly colored cotton. Unlike most other bangles, which advertise your approach with their racket and nearly cut off your circulation if you try to write, this one is light, flexible, soft, and silent, but by no means subdued. An armful of these bangles, as bright as a jar of jelly beans, would be unlikely to go unnoticed, and for very little outlay you could sport an impressive array of bracelets.

There are endless variations to explore. Try using fabric in shades of a single color, for example; you could take indigo and white, and use every kind of spot, check, stripe, or pattern that you can lay your hands on in those colors. Decorate your bangle with fancy ribbons or beads, or explore the potential of your sewing machine and try those old embroidery stitches that you have never found a use for. Because the raw materials cost almost nothing and the labor involved is minimal, making this bangle is a chance to be adventurous. If you are determined to be practical, you can always use washable fabrics and feel secure in the knowledge that you can put your bangle through the washing machine if it ever gets dirty.

**Scrap Circle**
*As bright and sassy as patchwork can be, this bangle flaunts the casual expertise with vivid color and playful piecing that comes after much experience with fabrics. Leave punctilious neatness for petit-point purses, and enjoy this piece for its exuberance.*

**Wrought Wrists**
*Made from a cheerful motley of different colors and kinds of fabric, punctuated by bright stitching, these bangles look good in great clashing armfuls.*

26

## Sewing the Bangle

*Spread out all your tattered remnants, and pick a
sizzling kaleidoscope of the brightest and best. Make sure
your bangle is big enough to squeeze your hand into.*

Brightly
colored fabric

String

Batting

Muslin

Sewing thread

Colored
cotton thread

Stranded
embroidery floss

Contrasting fabric,
cut on the bias

Plain fabric

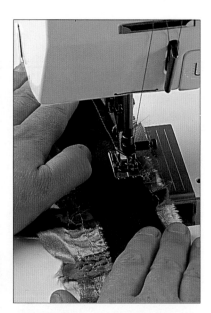

**1** *Cut out, or tear, small
rectangles of brightly colored fabric,
measuring approximately 3 X 1in
(7.5 X 2.5cm). Fraying the edges will
add texture to the bangle. Pin the
fabric scraps on to a strip of muslin
approximately 12in (30cm) long.
Layer them on top of each other to
build up a richly decorated surface.*

**2** *Thread a sewing machine with
colored cotton thread. With the
machine on free-motion embroidery,
stitch across the fabric patches in
different directions to attach them
to the strip of muslin.*

**3** *With right sides together, pin
and stitch the outer edge of a
strip of plain fabric down one side of
the patched strip. Stitch a second plain
strip to the other side of the patched
strip. Fold back the two plain strips
to reveal a 1in (2.5cm) wide area of
pattern in the center of the patched
strip, bordered with plain fabric. Trim
the edges of the colored fabric.*

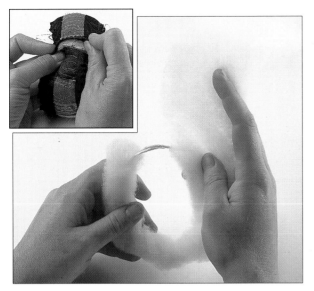

**4** *Make a double loop of string large enough for your hand to pass through, with a little extra. Knot the loop. Wrap batting around the loop. Stitch the end in place to prevent the batting from unraveling. Wrap the patched strip around the outer edge of the padded loop, and slipstitch the ends together with sewing thread (see inset).*

**5** *Using sewing thread, stitch the two inner edges of the patched strip to the bangle, stitching through the batting and pulling the thread tightly. The fabric will begin to pucker, but continue to stitch as evenly as possible. Cut out a strip of contrasting fabric approximately 10in (25cm) long and 2in (5cm) wide.*

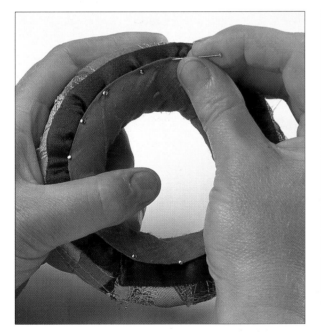

**6** *Turn under the edge of the contrasting fabric, pin this around the inner edge of the bangle to conceal the stitches made in step 5 and part of the plain fabric edges. Stretching the fabric as you go, pin it at short intervals, sticking the pins down into the batting. Repeat on the other side of the bangle, so the fabric fits smoothly around the inside. Slipstitch the contrasting fabric in place.*

**7** *Thread a needle with a contrasting color of stranded embroidery floss. Sew the edges of the two plain-colored fabrics together with a tiny running stitch, pinching the edges together as you go.*

# Felt Baubles

**MATERIALS**
Predyed fleece
Laundry soap powder
Water
Nylon-coated
miniature wire cable
Necklace finding
Crimp beads

**EQUIPMENT**
Bowl
Craft knife
Needle
Long-nosed pliers
Wire cutters

**W**OOL IS A VERY UNLIKELY component of jewelry, but these giant felt beads have an unexpected extrovert appeal. The color is so rich, the texture so dense, the completed item so light to wear, and so dramatic to look at, that you may have to reconsider all your preconceptions as to what constitutes jewelry.

There is a mysterious aspect to the making of these marbled, woolen ping-pong balls; you will discover the strange desire of wool fibers to turn themselves into perfect spheres. You will also end up with very clean hands indeed. The wool you use is available predyed in a range of rich colors. To make a necklace, simply alternate one or two different-colored beads, or create a whole rainbow. For variety, use different sizes of woolen balls in partnership with each other, or embellish them with regularly spaced or patterned sequins and tiny pins, studs, or beads. You could cut them in half, and either use them with their swirling middles exposed or pair them with a different-colored hemisphere to make a bicolored ball.

**Sharp Spheres**
*Viridian, magenta, and black make a startling trio that perfectly suits a snappy sophisticated look. Just pair a sleek black suit with an unmistakable designer look with these brilliant baubles, and you will make an impression wherever you go.*

**Black and White and Round All Over**
*Black and white always look good together, and these swirling felt beads are no exception — they would look perfect worn with plain, bright colors, or subtle autumnal shades.*

## Making the Collar

*This necklace is a winter adornment — it is comfortingly warm to wear, and a lot of fun to make.*

Necklace finding

Crimp beads

Nylon-coated miniature wire cable

Laundry soap powder

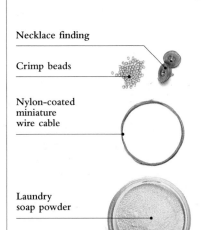

Predyed fleece

**1** *Pull a piece of fleece, about 6in (15cm) long, off a hank of predyed green fleece. Wrap it together with a similar-size piece of pink fleece, twisting the two colors together in your hands to combine them. Wrap them around and around to make a tight ball. Put on one side. Repeat to make about 15 balls.*

**2** *Pull several thin strands of black fleece off a hank, and wrap them individually around some of the pink and green balls for added decoration. Repeat the process with thin strands of pink and green fleece, if desired. Do not worry about securing the ends; these will be matted together when the fleece is made into felt.*

**3** *Mix laundry soap powder with hot water in a bowl until the water is very bubbly. Dip a fleece ball into the soapy water, then rub it between your hands to turn it into felt. Rub it gently at first, then gradually increase the pressure, dipping the ball into the soapy water periodically to keep it moist. When the ball is hard and compact, and you are no longer able to squeeze it, it is ready. This takes at least 15 minutes per ball. Repeat with each fleece ball.*

**4** *Rinse the felt balls in clear water, squeezing out the bubbles. Keep changing the water in the bowl, or rinse the balls under running water. Continue to rinse until all the bubbles have been washed out.*

**5** *Using a craft knife, cut a few of the felt balls in half. The open halves will reveal the patterns made by the different colors of fleece.*

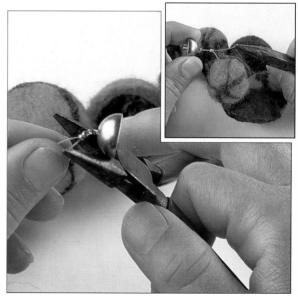

**6** *Unroll a length of nylon-coated miniature wire cable and, without cutting it off the roll, thread it through the eye of a needle. Thread the needle through one half of a necklace finding. Next take the needle through two crimp beads to thread them on to the wire, butting them up against the necklace finding. Then push the needle through the center of each felt bead and half-bead, in turn, to wire the beads together to make the necklace.*

**7** *Thread on two crimp beads, then the other half of the necklace finding. Bend the wire back and trim the wire with wire cutters at each end of the necklace. At each end, push the crimp beads down toward the finding, over the cut end of the wire, so they butt up against the finding (see inset). Using pliers, flatten the crimp beads to secure them. Snip off the end of the wire with wire cutters to neaten the necklace.*

# Magic Earrings

## MATERIALS

Vanishing muslin
Machine
embroidery threads
Metallic thread
Strong cotton thread
in outline color
Variety of small beads
Gold-plated
jewelry wire
2 gold ear wires

## EQUIPMENT

Felt-tip pen
Sewing machine
and darning foot
Old towel
Iron
Sharp sewing scissors
Fine or
beading needle
Wire cutters
Round-nosed pliers

THE MAGIC IN THIS CASE is a product of technology. The rich, shimmering fabric of these earrings speckled with gold and silver beads is simply a fine lacy web of machine stitching, from which the dull backing fabric has been burned away. (An alternative disappearing backing fabric, featured on pp. 44–5, dissolves in water.) This technique introduces a new arena of design, because you are actually creating your fabric from threads – and seeing the muslin vanish is as close to magic as jewelry can get. As you become proficient with the technique, you can tackle larger and more intricate pieces; the designer who created these earrings also makes elaborate collars, brooches, and hat pins.

To see the breathtaking polychrome potential of stitching your own fabric, you only have to admire the glossy spectrum of colored embroidery threads that beckons from any notions counter. You can choose any combination of colors under the sun, and experiment with different kinds of thread, from silk and cotton flosses to metallic. The finished earrings are light, glamorous, and a pleasure to wear.

**Beaded Pageantry**
*These earrings have an air of medieval finery. Their charm comes from a simple design intricately finished, and from the strong harmonious colors of the stitching.*

**Intricate Stitches**
*Made with the same basic ingredients – vanishing muslin with a fine overlay of machine stitches and tiny, brightly colored beads – these embroidered earrings have subtly different effects, depending on their shape and color.*

## Embroidering the Earrings

*It's a good idea to practice stitching before
you commit yourself to hours of patient machine-stitching.
The beads are easy to attach, and give a delicate finish.*

Metallic thread

Vanishing muslin

Strong cotton thread in outline color

Gold-plated jewelry wire

Gold earring wires

Variety of small beads

Machine embroidery threads

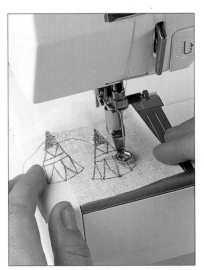

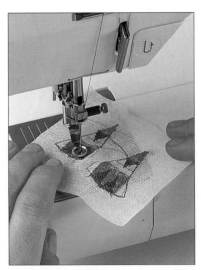

**1** *Using a pen, draw your earring design on to a piece of vanishing muslin. It is best to stick to simple shapes, such as triangles or squares, to begin with, because they are easier to stitch. As you become more confident, you can tackle more intricate shapes. Decide which colors you will be using in the design; a limited palette of three or four colors, at most, produces the best results.*

**2** *Thread the sewing machine with the first color of machine embroidery thread; set it for straight stitch. Keep the feed dog down when stitching. Using the darning foot, stitch the upper area of the design by building up layers of thread. Try to develop a rhythm between your hand movements and the machine speed, because this prevents the machine from jamming; you will need to practice.*

**3** *Continue to fill areas of the design with the first color of machine embroidery thread. Rethread the machine with a second color, and stitch more areas of the design in the same way.*

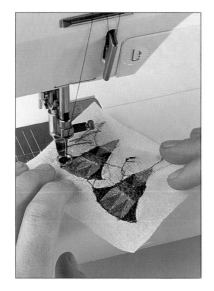

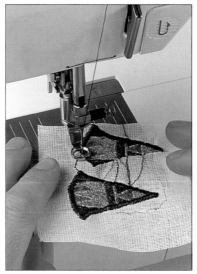

**4** *Continue to stitch the design using more colors of thread, until all areas of the design have been filled. This design uses only four colors of thread, but they are rich colors that all work well together.*

**5** *Using metallic thread, overstitch between colors within the design using a tight zigzag stitch. Thread the machine with an outline color, and using a wider zigzag, overstitch the outline of the design.*

**6** *Place the stitched muslin face down on an old towel. Iron the muslin with a very hot iron until it turns a burned brown color. Muslin burns at a lower temperature than thread. Let the muslin cool.*

**7** *When the muslin has cooled, rub it between your hands and the muslin will flake away, leaving the stitched threads intact. Pull off any remaining pieces of muslin with your fingers, and trim loose threads with a pair of sharp scissors.*

**8** *Thread a fine or beading needle with a doubled strong cotton thread in an outline color. Make a few stitches in the back of one earring to fasten the thread, then stitch small beads on to each earring. To finish, make a few stitches in the back of the earring, then snip off the thread.*

**9** *Cut a 1¼in (3cm) length of wire with wire cutters. Insert one end in the top of one earring; make a loop at the end with round-nosed pliers. Thread three beads on to the wire; make a loop with the remaining wire (see inset). Attach the ear wire with pliers; repeat with the second earring.*

# Kaleidoscope Necklet

## MATERIALS

Newspaper
Wallpaper paste
White latex paint
Water-based
gouache paints
Oil-based
polyurethane varnish
Cord
Jump ring and clasp
Wooden beads

## EQUIPMENT

Wire rack
Artist's brushes
Knitting needles
Small dish
Scissors

A RESPLENDENT EXAMPLE of the wonders that can be achieved at very little cost, this rainbow necklet can be made with the most basic materials – sheets of newspaper and wallpaper paste. Papier-mâché is a very amenable material, and having made a brilliant Matisse-bright necklace, you could try variations. Experiment with enormous beads (modeled around ping-pong balls), dangling hearts, spheres, cubes, and ovals. Try several strands together for an African-inspired collar, or create a napoleon of flat circles threaded close together.

The cheapness and easy availability of the materials mean that you can afford to experiment, and ditch your disasters. You could turn out a Christmas choker in holly colors with touches of tinsel, a wedding special in white and gold, or a spectacular Carmen Miranda-style necklace in fabulous fruit shapes. On the other hand, baubles with a smooth finish and subtle colors to match a favorite dress would give you instant sophistication on a shoestring.

**Paper Rainbow**
*This necklet is unabashed fun; its primary colors and knobbly tactile shapes have the air of a Mexican fiesta and give a decided lift to the spirits. Wooden spacer beads echo the primary colors.*

**Confetti Colors**
*Painted paper beads can exhibit any image you like – stripes, spots, and even faces. Here, newspaper is the background for muted color, and metal links give an airy look.*

## Making the Beads

*Having read the Sunday papers, you can tear
them to shreds. Forget about the bad news and create
your own pulp fantasy instead.*

Wallpaper paste

White
latex paint

Newspaper

Water-based
gouache paints

Wooden beads

Oil-based
polyurethane
varnish

Bolt ring
and clasp

Cord

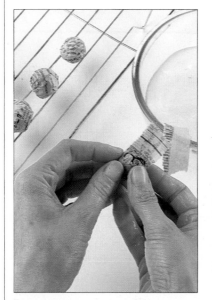

**1** *Tear newspaper into small pieces,
approximately 5 X 2in (12.5 X
5cm). Dip one piece in wallpaper
paste, and scrunch it up to make a
round ball shape. Cover with smaller
pieces of paper and smooth down.
Repeat to make a total of 17 shapes,
ranging in size, and place them on
a wire rack to dry for 48 hours.*

**2** *Using an artist's brush, paint
each "bead" with a coat of white
latex paint. This covers the newspaper
and provides a plain, smooth surface
to decorate. Let the painted beads dry
on the wire rack for at least two hours.*

**3** *Push four or five of the beads on
to a knitting needle, spacing them
approximately 1in (2.5cm) apart, to
enable you to decorate them on all
sides at once.*

**4** *Using water-based gouache paint, decorate the beads with a range of multicolored squiggles, stripes, and dots. Prop the knitting needle over a shallow bowl, and let the beads dry for two hours.*

**5** *Take the dry beads off the needle. Replace one bead at a time on the needle, and dip it into a can of varnish. Flick the excess varnish on to newspaper, then let the beads dry on the wire rack for approximately five hours.*

**6** *Arrange the beads in the order of threading, with the largest beads in the center, and the smallest ones at the two ends. Cut a long length of cord. Tie one end of the cord on to the bolt ring, leaving a long end. Starting at one end of the necklet, thread the cord through the beads, alternating paper beads with wooden beads.*

**7** *When you have threaded on the last bead, tie the clasp securely on to the end of the cord. Rethread the long end, which was left when attaching the bolt ring, back through a few of the beads to hide it. Trim off the visible end of the cord to neaten.*

# Renaissance Riches

## MATERIALS

Brightly colored silk

Hot-water-
dissolvable fabric

Metallic threads

Vinyl

Machine
embroidery threads

Colored
cotton threads

Cardboard

Silk lining

Water

Fine gauze fabric

Velvet

Metallic silk

Variety of beads

Goldwork
metallic pieces

Brass wire,
¹⁄₁₆in (1mm) thick

Epoxy adhesive

Hat pin

## EQUIPMENT

Scissors

Pins

Sewing machine

Deep-sided bowl

Kettle

Needle

Embroidery hoop

Fine sewing scissors

Wire cutters

Round-nosed pliers

THIS INTRICATE HAT PIN, which exploits many techniques and is enriched by sumptuous encrustations of color and texture, might well have embellished the headband of a Medici beauty. The magical transition from basic raw materials to a finished work of art is extraordinary, and relies on layering of embroidery, fabric, beading, and metal curlicues. The steps are a little tedious, but none is complicated in itself, and the result is refined and ethereal with a subtlety of color and a fascinating texture that demand closer inspection.

Part of the pleasure of making this hat pin derives from using vanishing muslin as a base; in this case, boiling water was used to dissolve the backing fabric (see pp.36–7, where the backing is burned away). This piece is the outcome of much experimentation with different layers and fabrics. After you have mastered all the stages, you could incorporate metallic gauze, lace, or ribbon, and add different beads.

**Filigree Stitching**
*This hat pin, which might easily have graced the feathered cockade of any self-respecting cavalier, is an essential accessory to transform the plain and everyday with a theatrical touch of splendor.*

**Pin Spectacular**
*These unusually shaped hat pins can take anything that a pack-rat imagination can dream up, such as extra colored beads, more wire, or added free-falling dangles.*

42

## Assembling the Hat Pin

*Collect all your bright silk scraps together,*
*and try out the effect of different fabrics and colors with*
*one another. Finish with your most glamorous beads.*

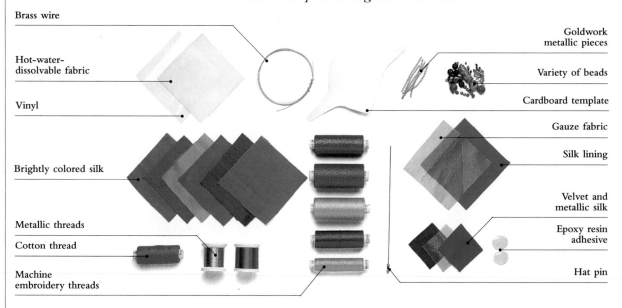

Brass wire

Hot-water-dissolvable fabric

Vinyl

Brightly colored silk

Metallic threads

Cotton thread

Machine embroidery threads

Goldwork metallic pieces

Variety of beads

Cardboard template

Gauze fabric

Silk lining

Velvet and metallic silk

Epoxy resin adhesive

Hat pin

**1** *Cut out several small squares of brightly colored silk, and lay them out on top of a piece of hot-water-dissolvable fabric so they cover it entirely. Sprinkle some short lengths of metallic thread over the top. Place a piece of vinyl on top of the threads, and pin to secure.*

**2** *Prepare your sewing machine for free-motion running stitch, threading gold machine embroidery thread in the top and a contrasting cotton thread in the bobbin. Loosen the bobbin tension. When you begin stitching, the bottom thread should be brought up so it lies on the surface of the fabric, creating a knobbly effect. Stitch over the vinyl in a pattern of loops and squiggles.*

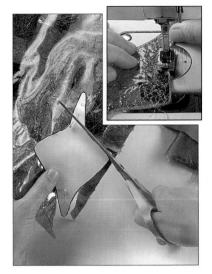

**3** Make a cardboard template of the fabric shape. Pin it to the embroidered fabric; cut out the shape. Cut out the same shape from the silk lining. Stitch the embroidered piece to the lining, with the vinyl facing upward. Trim off excess silk. Using metallic and cotton threads, zigzag stitch around the shape (see inset).

**4** Lay the embroidered piece in a deep-sided bowl. Pour boiling water over the top to submerge the piece. The hot-water-dissolvable fabric will shrink, making the vinyl bubble up. Remove the piece after a few seconds, when it stops moving and shrinking. Rinse in cold water, then squeeze out any excess. Let dry.

**5** Twist the long ends of the piece, and fold them in toward the center of the design. Pin in position, leaving a section clear for the metal hat pin to be threaded through at the top and bottom, then hand-stitch the ends down to secure.

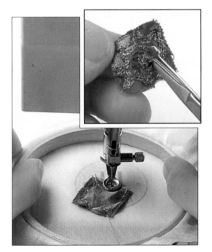

**6** Insert the gauze in an embroidery hoop. Place a small square of velvet in the hoop, then add a square of silk and two squares of metallic silk on top. Using contrasting metallic threads, stitch a spiral pattern over the squares in free-motion running stitch. Remove the stitched squares from the hoop. Using embroidery scissors, cut away some of the silk to reveal the velvet between the stitching (see inset).

**7** Stitch the embroidered velvet square to the center of the main piece, sewing a bead in with each stitch. Then decorate the piece with a variety of different-shaped beads and goldwork metallic pieces, attaching each of them with a few small stitches.

**8** Cut two 3¼in (9cm) lengths of brass wire with wire cutters. Using round-nosed pliers, bend the wires into two small spiral shapes. Stitch these to the back of the piece, so they protrude at each side. Glue a large bead on to the end of the hat pin with epoxy resin adhesive. When dry, thread the pin through the gaps in the top and bottom of the embroidered piece.

# Ideas to Inspire

Paper and fabric jewelry is all about magic. Now that you have seen the amazing range of techniques and the fabulous results which can be exacted from the most humble and universally available materials, we show many more wonders on these pages, using the same simple elements.

Even the most parsimonious would-be jeweler will not begrudge a foray into the fabric scrap bag or wastepaper basket, and the most cautious surely cannot resist the temptation to experiment, especially when the results can be this spectacular!

**▼ Miniature Vegetables**
*A cauliflower brooch and Brussels sprout earrings are made from hand-dyed silk taffeta and organza, glued to a Styrofoam base. The center of the cauliflower is made from tiny beads.*

**▲ Radical Radishes**
*Cotton balls dyed with fabric dye were used to make this radish hat pin and the earrings. The leaves were made from hand-dyed wired silk, and attached to the radishes by a wired cord stalk. A radish was wired to each ear hook; one was glued to a hat pin.*

**► Heart Beads**
*These tiny heart earrings are made from red velvet decorated with shiny gold machine embroidery and blue beads.*

**◄ Dramatic Plastic**
*Garbage bags, blue plastic bags, and old potato chip bags are recycled to make these striking hand-hooked earrings. The large, floppy loops on the silver earrings give the pieces extra pizzazz.*

46

◀ **Silver Lace**
*These delicate earrings were machine-embroidered with metallic thread on water-soluble dissolvable fabric. The more open, lacy stitches of the star earrings were laminated in plastic for protection.*

▲ **Paper Triangles**
*Decorated with a combination of printing techniques, and gold, silver, and copper powders, the paper for these pins was pieced together to create rich layers of patterning.*

▼ **Deeply Felt**
*Made with predyed woolen fleece, felted with laundry soap powder, these chunky necklaces will make a brilliant impact on a gray day. The addition of studs (bottom) transforms a couple of stripey felt balls into earrings.*

◀ **Literary Links**
*Inspired by William Shakespeare, these wooden brooches and cuff links were decorated with decoupage from color photocopies.*

### ▶ Stitched Silk
These padded and stuffed silk earrings and brooch are embellished with appliqué and rich stitch-work techniques, using shiny rayon threads, to create intricate decoration and intense color.

### ▲ Tubular Beads
Made with pieces of clear plastic tubing cut to different lengths, this necklace is decorated with colored threads and strung together with gold silk cord. Some of the pieces of tubing have been scored to create textural indentations.

### ◀ Paper Disks
To make these earrings, small disks were cut from handmade textured paper, decorated with gouache paint and gold ink, and sealed. The colored disks were then threaded onto wire, along with papier-mâché beads.

### ▼ Paper and Silk
These colorful necklaces combine rolled paper tubes with silver-plated and wooden beads and silk. The tubes were made from screen-printed paper, with added sponged and brushed color, and copper, silver, and gold powders for extra richness and depth.

### ▶ Studded Brooches
Made from tiny pieces of newspaper layered over shaped cardboard, these papier-mâché pins are decorated with pieces of mirror glass, colored glitter, beads, and gold paint.

### ▼ Hearts and Stars

*Hearts, moons, and stars are popular motifs in jewelry. These earrings are made from papier-mâché decorated with flat-backed gemstones and candy wrappers (below), and paints (right).*

### ▼ Gilded Paper

*To create these intriguing pieces, layers of sketch paper were laminated with white craft glue and decorated with acrylic paints, gilding metals, and creams. The pieces were then scratched and embossed.*

### ▶ Beaded Stitchery

*Created by intricate machine-embroidery over vanishing muslin, this stitched pendant is further embellished with tiny copper, gold, and amber beads. The pendant is hung on a wrapped, beaded cord.*

# Bead and Glass Jewelry

························

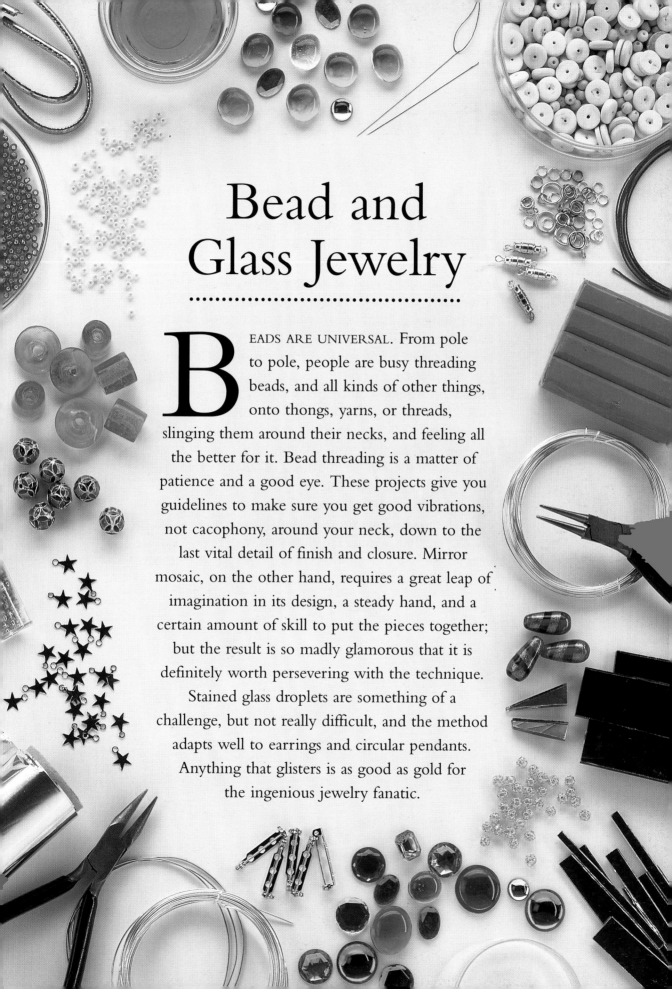

**B**EADS ARE UNIVERSAL. From pole to pole, people are busy threading beads, and all kinds of other things, onto thongs, yarns, or threads, slinging them around their necks, and feeling all the better for it. Bead threading is a matter of patience and a good eye. These projects give you guidelines to make sure you get good vibrations, not cacophony, around your neck, down to the last vital detail of finish and closure. Mirror mosaic, on the other hand, requires a great leap of imagination in its design, a steady hand, and a certain amount of skill to put the pieces together; but the result is so madly glamorous that it is definitely worth persevering with the technique. Stained glass droplets are something of a challenge, but not really difficult, and the method adapts well to earrings and circular pendants. Anything that glisters is as good as gold for the ingenious jewelry fanatic.

# Millefiori Mosaic Beads

**MATERIALS**

Polymer clay
Seed beads
Gold-plated
jewelry wire

**EQUIPMENT**

Craft knife
Rolling pin
Needle
Baking sheet
Oven
Wire cutters
Round-nosed pliers

POLYMER CLAY is another miracle of modern technology. In addition to being colorful and malleable, it also keeps its shape after a brief baking. If your childhood was spent rolling endless playdough snakes, you will have a head start for this more refined kindergarten pastime, which could have the same therapeutic effect as kneading bread dough. As you become proficient at the rolling techniques involved, you can then progress to making beads of great delicacy and sophistication.

A limited palette tends to look better than a jazzy motley of brilliant colors. Black and white beads can look chic, as can the earth colors of Aboriginal "dreaming" paintings. Parchment and indigo are also an attractive combination. Making this project is an ideal occasion to enlist the help of young children, but keep in mind that you have to be cautious with the fumes that polymer clay produces on baking, so open all the windows for this stage. Some people have discovered that turning up the oven to a really high heat for the last ten minutes or so of baking gives the finished beads a shiny, almost ceramic, look.

**Fired with Enthusiasm**
*It takes practice to achieve this deft touch with detail, but the learning experience is a pleasurable one, and your creations will be entirely original. Be patient, and look at books on mosaics for inspiration.*

**Wrap and Roll**
*After you have mastered the basic techniques of using polymer clay, it is child's play to make a pair of earrings to match your necklace.*

52

## Making the Beads

*Find a handful of pretty colors, flex your
creative muscles, and get to work.*

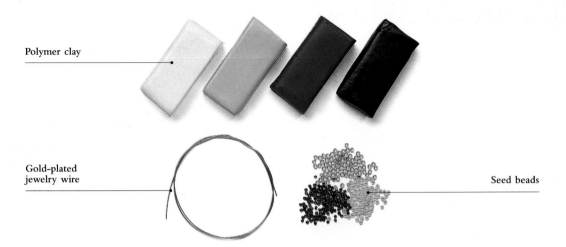

Polymer clay

Gold-plated
jewelry wire

Seed beads

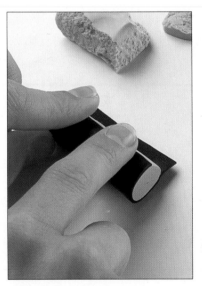

**1** *Soften half a block of black
polymer clay by kneading it for
several minutes on a work surface.
Soften half a block of white polymer
clay in the same way. Flatten a thin
sheet of each color, roll them smooth
with a rolling pin, then trim the edges
with a craft knife to make rectangles.
Place the white rectangle on top of
the black rectangle, roll them with a
rolling pin to remove any air bubbles,
then carefully roll them up to form
a spiral log. Set aside.*

**2** *To make a wrapped log, knead
a block of first black, then beige,
polymer clay until pliable. Make a log
shape with beige clay. Wrap this log
with a very thin sheet of black clay.
Trim the edges of the black clay where
they meet, so the edges butt up
exactly and do not overlap. Roll the
wrapped log gently with your fingers
to consolidate the shape. Set aside.*

**3** *Next, make a striped log. First
knead a piece each of terra-cotta,
beige, white, and black polymer clay
separately to soften, then roll each
piece into a square sheet. Lay them
one on top of the other in a stack.
Press down evenly to consolidate the
block, and trim the edges with a craft
knife. Cut the block in half, and place
one half on top of the other. Press
down again, thinning the stripes.
Repeat the process until the stripes
are as thin as desired. Set aside.*

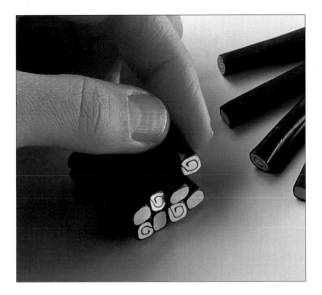

**4** To make a checkerboard log, square the ends of a spiral log (see step 1) and a wrapped log (see step 2) with your fingers. Elongate both logs by smoothing each side with your thumb and index finger. Cut four pieces from each log and stack them to form a checkerboard pattern. Compress this new log by rolling each side evenly.

**5** Take the striped block (see step 3) and slice it thickly with a craft knife. Lay these pieces around a piece of the black-and-white spiral log, with the stripes running lengthways. Roll this log to smooth out the seams and reduce its diameter.

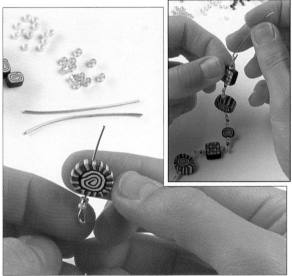

**6** Take all the patterned logs and use a craft knife to slice off as many beads as you need for a necklace. Each bead should be at least ¼in (5mm) thick to allow for piercing. Using a needle, pierce each of the beads (see inset). Piercing from one side to the middle, then from the other side to the middle, will help to center the hole. Place the beads on a baking sheet, and bake at 265°F (135°C) for approximately 30–45 minutes.

**7** Assemble the necklace by threading polymer clay beads together with seed beads on to gold-plated wire. Cut a 2in (5cm) length of wire with wire cutters. Loop one end of the wire with round-nosed pliers, and thread on two seed beads, then one polymer clay bead. Then, thread on two more seed beads, and make a loop in the top of the wire to secure. Loop the next length of wire through this loop (see inset), and thread on beads, as above. Repeat to make the necklace as long as you like. Join up the two ends by looping two adjoining wires.

# Stained Glass Pendant

**MATERIALS**

Paper
Colored glass
Channeled lead
Glass nugget
Flux
Solder
Bolt ring
Chain

**EQUIPMENT**

Black felt-tip pen
Glass cutter
Square-nosed pliers
Lead knife
Fid (see p.10)
Soldering iron

NOTHING ELSE has quite the same intense color as stained glass. It casts a luminous glow whenever the light catches it. Just think of cathedral windows tracing a bright rainbow on the nave and you will appreciate how sumptuous and special glass can be. Its unique transparency and color make it a particularly exciting material to use. When you start to look carefully, you will notice that colored glass can have differing qualities. Some is smoothly even, and some is ribbed and rippled in a fascinating way. A little familiarity with the glass cutter and soldering iron might suggest other possibilities. Using mirror glass, for example, creates flashes of light and a sparkle that is irresistible: people always comment on mirror jewelry.

In addition to making brooches, pendants, and earrings, you could stray into the realms of interior decoration and experiment with making adornments for light fixtures and candlesticks. Before you know it, you will be captivated by glassblowers' and glaziers' waste materials, and broken pieces of colored, pressed, or engraved glass will become thrilling additions to your jewelry collection.

**Light Fantastic**
*Like a miniature stained glass window, this glass pendant casts wonderfully colorful shadows. Fortunately, no one has yet thought to put a tax on pure light and color, so you can indulge in these luxuries extravagantly.*

**Shapely Shards**
*You will never get tired of simple permutations of shape and color when working with glass because of its peculiarly seductive quality. Glass is color at its most pure.*

## Making the Pendant

*Experiment with your soldering iron until you feel
familiar with it and can control the magical transformation
of dull metal by burnishing with heat.*

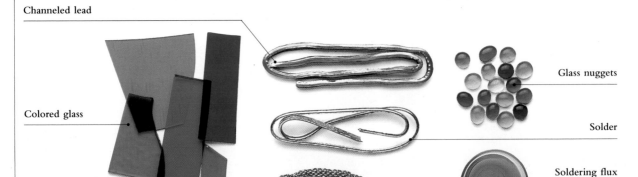

Channeled lead

Colored glass

Chain

Glass nuggets

Solder

Soldering flux

Bolt ring

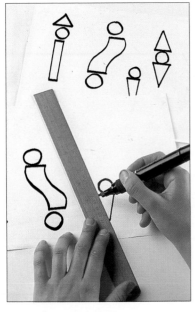

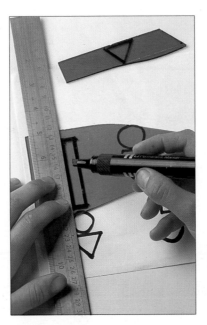

**1** *Using a black felt-tip pen and ruler, draw out a design for your pendant on paper. Stick with simple shapes, such as triangles, rectangles, and diamonds; these are easier to cut out of glass. Circles are difficult to cut from a piece of glass, but you can use glass nuggets instead.*

**2** *Decide on the colors of glass you want to use for each element of the pendant. Then lay a piece of colored glass over each of the drawn shapes in turn, and trace the shapes on to the glass using a black felt-tip pen and a ruler.*

**3** *Cut out the shapes drawn on the glass using a glass cutter. Cut either inside or outside the outline for all pieces, but be consistent. Holding the glass cutter upright, push it away from you, keeping your hand steady. When you have started cutting along a line do not stop until you reach the end, because the glass could splinter off and result in an uneven edge.*

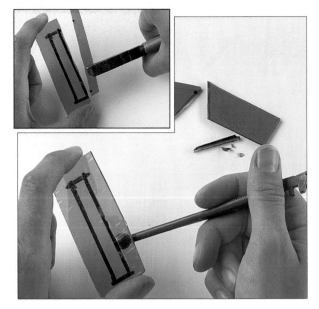

4 *When you have cut around the drawn shape, tap gently on the underside of the glass along the scored line, with the ball of the glass cutter. Holding the glass firmly in one hand, use square-nosed pliers to grip the glass close to the scored line and pull it away. The glass should break in one piece and come away in the pliers (see inset). If it does not break off, repeat the tapping and pulling. Cut out all the pieces for the pendant in the same way.*

5 *Take a length of channeled lead and wrap it around each of the glass sections of the pendant, including the glass nugget. Channeled lead is flexible and will wrap easily. Cut off the spare lead using a lead knife. Because lead is fairly soft, cutting it feels like cutting through cheese. To secure the glass, press the lead into the sides of the glass using a fid (see inset). Repeat with all sections of the pendant.*

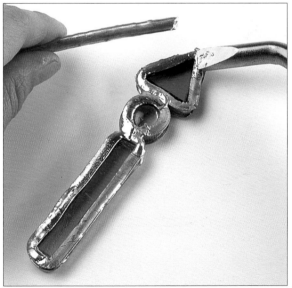

6 *Solder the sections of the pendant together. To do this, first apply flux on the joints with a paintbrush, then solder with a soldering iron, following the manufacturer's instructions. Hold the stick of solder on the joint, then touch this with the soldering iron. The solder will melt into the joints, welding the pieces together.*

7 *Run the solder around the lead to give it a silver appearance. Then solder a bolt ring on the end of, and at right angles to, the pendant. Let the pendant cool, then wash it in dishwashing liquid to remove the flux. Rinse and let dry. Finally, thread a chain through the bolt ring to complete the pendant.*

# Four-Stranded Necklace

**MATERIALS**
Silver-plated
jewelry wire
Very fine fuse wire
Assorted beads
Black polyester thread
Superglue

**EQUIPMENT**
Wire cutters
Round-nosed pliers
Scissors
Needle

THERE IS A FINE ART to putting beads together. To the uninitiated it may seem that a necklace virtually assembles itself, but when you get down to it, you will find that the beads you thought were destined for a long and harmonious relationship do not do anything for one another when placed side by side, and those you wanted to discard are perfect partners for your favorites. There are some magnificent bead catalogs available, which make the whole process of choosing beads easier, though nothing really beats feeling, weighing, and trying one particular bead with another.

Colors and quantities are just a matter of taste and experience, but to start with, it is comforting to have some guidance. If your beads look good in a heap, they will look good when threaded together; in this instance, there is a cohesive common denominator of color and material. Glass beads tend to be the most expensive, but they also have an enduring shine and inimitable glowing transparency.

**Threaded Treasure**
*This sophisticated, dressy necklace is colored with shades of glowing berry reds, marbled with black, and given a touch of silver. Different beads give very different looks; shiny glass, faceted crystal, or glinting metal are all sophisticated, while matte glass, dark antiqued metal, dull brass or copper, and wood are more casual.*

**Venerable Beads**
*Both these necklaces have beads of roughly similar scale and color for a balanced effect.*

## Threading the Beads

*Choose beads in a limited range of colors, and*
*add a touch of contrast in silver or gold.*

Black polyester thread

Assorted beads

Silver-plated jewelry wire

Very fine fuse wire

Superglue

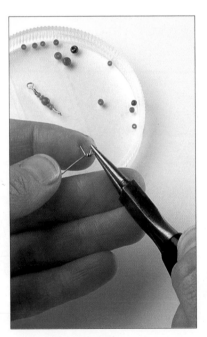

**1** Using wire cutters, cut a piece of silver-plated jewelry wire about 2½in (6cm) long. Using round-nosed pliers, make a small loop in the wire, then coil the rest of the wire at right angles to the loop to make a tight coil. Repeat the process to make 11 more wire coils. Set aside.

**2** Cut a piece of very fine fuse wire about 2½–3¼in (6–8cm) long. Make a tiny loop at one end with round-nosed pliers. Thread three or four small beads on to the wire. Then, using the pliers, fold the top of the wire back on itself to secure the beads. Repeat the process to make seven more beaded pieces.

**3** Cut four strands of black polyester thread, each approximately 40in (1m) long. Thread assorted beads on to the first strand, starting with a large decorative bead in the center. Make the strands of beads symmetrical, and choose beads in complementary colors. Leave approximately 12in (30cm) thread at each end.

**4** *Thread the other three strands with beads in a similar way, keeping the same color palette for all four strands and making sure that all the strands look good together. Intersperse the wire coils and beaded pieces (see steps 1 and 2) among the beads. Leave approximately 11½in (28.5cm) of thread at each end.*

**5** *Tie an 80in (2m) length of black polyester thread in a knot around the four threads at one end of the beaded strands. You should now have six trailing ends of thread. Thread all six strands of thread into a ¼in (5mm) bead, and push the bead up against the knot. Repeat this process with the four threads at the other end of the necklace.*

**6** *Divide the six threads at one end into three sections: a middle section consisting of the four original threads, and two longer threads, one on each side. To braid, take the left-hand thread under the middle threads, and over the right-hand thread. Then take the right-hand thread over the middle threads, and under the left-hand thread. Repeat down the length of the threads.*

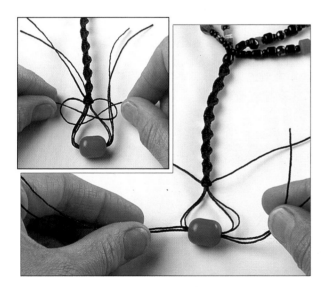 

**7** *Braid to within ¾in (2cm) of the end of the threads. The braiding will twist and tighten as you work. Then split the four middle threads into two, and thread them through a large bead, with two threads going into the bead from one side and the other two from the other side. Bring the thread ends back up toward the braiding, and tie the longer outer threads over them to secure (see inset). Braid the outer threads over the middle thread ends to neaten.*

**8** *Repeat step 6 with the other end of the necklace. Then braid the middle threads to make a buttonhole large enough to fit over the bead (see step 7). Fold these braided threads back to the braiding to create a loop. Tie the outer threads over the ends, then braid over the ends to neaten. Tidy the ends by threading them through the braiding three times with a needle (see inset). Trim the ends, then dab them with Superglue to secure.*

# Glittering Regalia

## MATERIALS

Paper
Colored mirror glass
Flat-backed
glass rhinestones
Aluminum foil
Fiberglass resin
Thin gauge wire
Pin back
Bolt rings
Water

## EQUIPMENT

Pen
Glass cutter
Long-nosed pliers
Tin snips
Protective mask
Small container
Toothpick
Craft knife
Adhesive putty
Wire cutters
Toothbrush

THIS IS THEATRICAL glamour *par excellence* and perfect for your own personal coronation, to commemorate some particularly daring exploit of an amatory or ambitious nature, or just for the 18-carat fun of it. This brooch is not for those who feel perfectly happy with a single strand of carefully graduated freshwater pearls; instead, this is a showy, glorious celebration of the joy of kitsch. It contains all the elements of a jeweler's repertoire of significant and seductive motifs – hearts, diamonds, teardrops, stars, crescents, and crosses – expressed in a royal ransom of chunks of glittering mirror glass.

It is all too often forgotten, in the curious human urge to flaunt its fortune, that jewelry is as much about fun and theater as it is about money, if not more so. This flamboyant piece takes a humorous and ironic outrageous angle on the whole matter of self-adornment. If you ever yearned to break the ice at parties, you will find that this is the decoration to do it. This brooch can be medal of honor for the shy, or a badge of predictable victory for the extroverted.

**Royal Flush**
*A study in scarlet and black, this elegantly bedizened brooch is to be worn with chutzpah and a broad smile. Alternatively, having mastered the intricacies of the mosaic brooch, you could treat the waiting world to a mosaic-spangled tiara.*

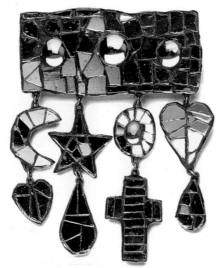

**Mirror Image**
*This brooch, made of faceted reflective mirror, sparkles with the same coruscations as the glittering gems that dazzle the eye at society galas, but without the cost.*

## Making the Brooch
*Enjoy the enormous range of finishes and
colors that is the province of glass alone, but treat glass
respectfully, since it can inflict injury.*

Aluminum foil

Paper

Fiberglass resin

Colored
mirror glass

Flat-backed glass
rhinestones

Plain mirror glass

Pin back

Bolt rings

Thin gauge wire

**1** *Draw a life-sized design for your brooch on paper. Using a glass cutter (see steps 3–4 on pp.58–59), cut colored mirror glass into strips. Then use long-nosed pliers and snips to break up the strips of mirror glass into smaller pieces.*

**2** *Assemble the pieces of glass, together with the flat-backed rhinestones, on top of the drawn design on the paper. Laying out the pieces on paper first allows you to change colors and adjust shapes as you go. Working on one part of the brooch at a time, transfer the mosaic pieces on to a square of aluminum foil. Position the pieces carefully, following the initial design.*

**3** *Work in a well-ventilated room and wear a protective mask because the fumes are very strong. Mix fiberglass resin in a small container using a toothpick. Dribble the resin around the mosaic edges with the toothpick. The resin will run underneath the glass pieces to form a pool on the aluminum foil. Keep teasing the pieces together with the toothpick.*

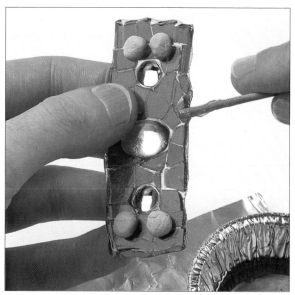

**4** The resin will take about 8 minutes to dry. Keep testing the edges. When it feels like thick gelatin, it is ready. Using a craft knife, cut around the edge of the brooch through the aluminum foil. Wait another few minutes for the resin to harden, then peel the foil off the back.

**5** Stick adhesive putty on the front of the brooch (this will keep it raised off the surface when you lay it down). Using a toothpick, apply liquid resin around the edges of the brooch. Place the brooch face-down on the aluminum foil so you can work on the back of it.

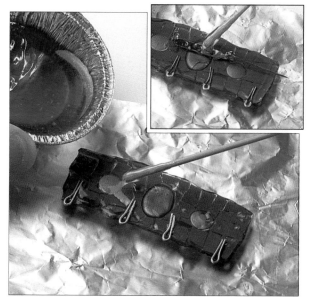

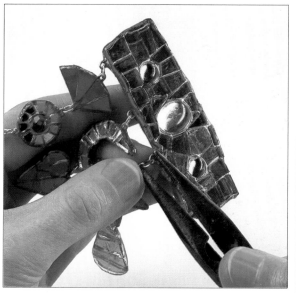

**6** Coat the back of the brooch with liquid resin. Then, using wire cutters, cut four pieces of wire, ¾in (2cm) long, and bend these into loops with pliers. Lay these wire loops along one long edge of the brooch bar, so the loops overhang the edge. Apply another coat of liquid resin over the wire loops to secure them in place. Position a pin back in the center of the brooch, on the opposite side to the loops. Seal with another coat of liquid resin (see inset). When dry, apply a final coat.

**7** Make the charms in the same way as the brooch bar, attaching wire loops to the top, then bolt rings to the loops to link the pieces. Open out the bolt rings with long-nosed pliers, and hook each one through a wire loop in the brooch bar to assemble the brooch. Squeeze the rings to close. Clean the front of the brooch by first dampening it with water, then scraping off any excess resin with a craft knife. Finally, scrub the front of the brooch with a toothbrush to remove any remaining traces of resin.

# Ideas to Inspire

Having dabbled with kindergarten materials such as paper, you may now wish to venture into more glamorous territory where glass and beads become your natural allies. This is the realm of glitz and kitsch, and all the more exciting for its heady mixture of sparkle and ingenuity. Take inspiration from the following pages and be bold and brash with your ideas. There is every reason to have fun with wild and wonderful creations.

▼ **Square Blocks**
*Polymer clay is the basis for these striking square earrings. The pattern was built up using seven colors of clay, then the squares were sliced off the block.*

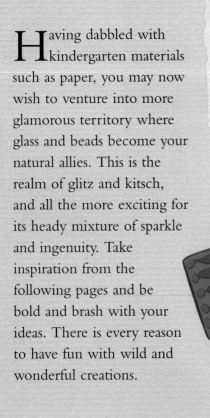

◄ **Sparkling Stars**
*Shards of mirror and smaller fragments of red glass were arranged together to form this dramatic star-shaped brooch and matching earrings. The glass is held together with a backing of several coats of resin.*

▶ **Indian Inspiration**
*Based on Indian motifs, these brooches were constructed from modeling clay built up in layers on cardboard shapes. Silver balls and beads, and tiny pieces of mirror, were inserted into the clay to add sparkle. Finally, the clay was painted.*

## ▼ Kitsch Cuffs

*These chunky bracelets are made from a base of twisted copper wire, through which strands of tiny colored beads are woven and secured with wire. Larger beads of glass, ceramic, plastic, and paper are interspersed throughout the pieces for added color and drama.*

## ▶ Diamanté Necklaces

*These glittering pendants are cast in plastic from molds in the shape of crosses, hearts, and stars. Holes are drilled in the plastic, and diamanté inserted and glued to fasten. Fine silver chains complete the pieces.*

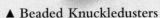

## ▲ Beaded Knuckledusters

*These silver rings are decorated with exuberant clusters of plastic beads and sparkling colored glass, threaded onto a silver wire base, which is then securely attached to the ring.*

## ▶ Planetary Influences

*Pieces of plain and colored mirror glass were cut with snips and arranged to create these dazzling designs, held together with layers of resin. Pin backs were embedded in the final layer.*

**◄ Thonged Beads**
*Simplicity works: a handful of natural-colored, stonewashed glass beads are threaded onto a fine leather thong. Knots tied in the leather between the beads hold them firmly in place.*

**◄ Threaded Pebbles**
*These necklaces are made using only natural materials. Pebbles are notched with a file, or a small hole is drilled at each side; then they are knotted together with waxed flax. Wooden beads give a contrast of texture.*

**◄ Sunburst Brooch**
*The center of this brooch is a seashell, onto which even-sized shards of mirror glass are soldered to represent a sunburst. The glass rays are also soldered to cover any sharp edges.*

70

▼ **Pipe Pieces**

*Inspired by Native American jewelry, these necklaces are made from pieces of broken clay pipe threaded onto string. Uncut semiprecious stones and a variety of small feathers were assembled together with silver wire to make up the pendants, creating the impression of little ziggurats.*

◄ **Moody Colors**

*Whether you make your own beads or buy them ready-made, polymer clay is a dream for creating simple necklaces. Use black and white for a sharp, crisp effect (above), or earthy tones (left) for warmth.*

71

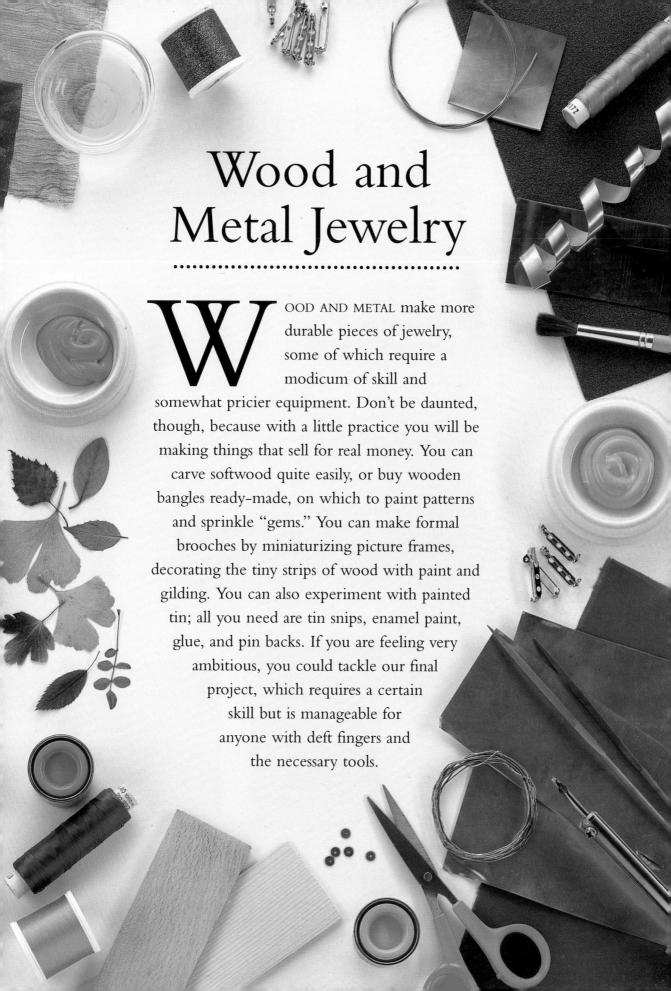

# Wood and Metal Jewelry

WOOD AND METAL make more durable pieces of jewelry, some of which require a modicum of skill and somewhat pricier equipment. Don't be daunted, though, because with a little practice you will be making things that sell for real money. You can carve softwood quite easily, or buy wooden bangles ready-made, on which to paint patterns and sprinkle "gems." You can make formal brooches by miniaturizing picture frames, decorating the tiny strips of wood with paint and gilding. You can also experiment with painted tin; all you need are tin snips, enamel paint, glue, and pin backs. If you are feeling very ambitious, you could tackle our final project, which requires a certain skill but is manageable for anyone with deft fingers and the necessary tools.

# Copper Leaf Brooch

## MATERIALS

Picture-framing glass,
⅛in (2mm) thick
Sheet copper
Acrylic paints
Pressed leaf
Polyvinyl white glue
Copper tape
Solder
Dishwashing liquid
Water
Superglue
Pin back

## EQUIPMENT

Metal ruler
Black felt-tip pen
Glass cutter
Scissors
Steel wool
2 artist's brushes
Soft cloth
Soldering iron

THIS PROFESSIONAL-LOOKING brooch makes an evocative country memento. It is easy to produce, using glass, copper tape, and an autumn leaf collected on a frosty morning walk and pressed between the pages of a telephone book. This particular leaf is from a gingko tree, but the fine leaves of aspen, maidenhair fern, rowan, or small oaks would all look equally good.

You could adapt this method – which illustrates, in effect, how to make a tiny picture frame – to show off other favorite souvenirs: a pressed flower, scraps of lace, and a ribbon to recollect a wedding; or a stamp, a graphic motif taken from the label of a particularly splendid bottle of wine, contour lines torn from a map, and the hamlet name to remember a vacation in France. Alternatively, if all this effort seems too fussy, you might find a ready-made image in a sheet of scraps, or a perfectly beautiful shell print in a moth-eaten thrift-store book on natural history. The point is that the autumn leaf is charming, and a pun is always fun, but anything flat and tiny will be shown off to advantage in its own miniature copper frame on a background of painted copper leaf.

### Grace from Fall

*Nature works hard to create beautiful things, and who are we to ignore them? Leaves make wonderful abstract works of art, come in myriad shapes and colors, cost nothing, and look ravishing in the right setting, as in this stylish brooch.*

### Pressed Leaves

*These four leaves, carefully pressed and meticulously decorated, are set against painted backgrounds that have a mysterious glow imparted by the copper leaf that subtly illuminates the color.*

## Assembling the Brooch

*Having pressed your leaf, think carefully about the
color of paint to use; red and green are boldly complementary,
while yellow glows against black.*

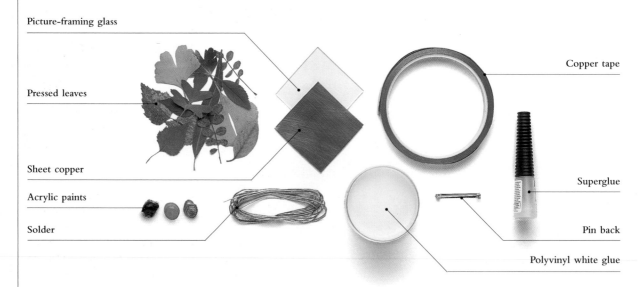

Picture-framing glass

Pressed leaves

Sheet copper

Acrylic paints

Solder

Copper tape

Superglue

Pin back

Polyvinyl white glue

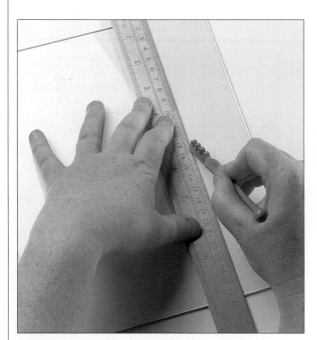

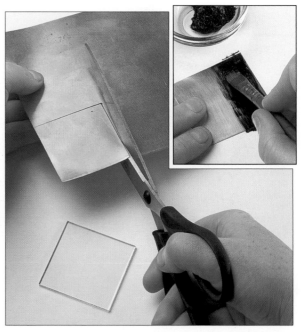

**1** *Take a piece of picture-framing glass, and measure
2in (5cm) in from one side at the top and bottom of
the piece. Mark with a felt-tip pen. Place a metal ruler
between the two pen marks, and holding it with one
hand, cut along the edge of the ruler with a glass cutter
(see steps 3–5 on pp.58–9). Then cut a 2in (5cm)
square from the glass strip in the same way.*

**2** *Place the glass square on a piece of sheet copper.
Draw around the edge with a black felt-tip pen.
Cut out the marked square with scissors. Rub the copper
square with steel wool to score it slightly so the paint can
adhere. Paint two or three coats of black acrylic paint over
the square (see inset), allowing each coat to dry before
applying the next, and let dry.*

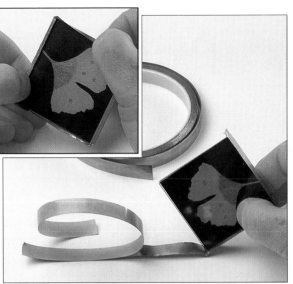

**3** *Select a nicely shaped pressed leaf that will fit within the black painted square. Decorate the leaf with gold and red acrylic paint using an artist's brush. Here, the leaf has been decorated with spots of color, but you can choose any pattern you like. Let dry for 5–10 minutes.*

**4** *To assemble the brooch, use white glue to stick the decorated leaf centrally on to the black square, and let dry. Then polish the glass square with a soft cloth and place it on top of the leaf. Cut a length of copper tape to fit around the edges of the square. Peel the sticky layer off the tape, and roll the square down the middle of the tape. Fold the copper tape down flat over the edges of the glass, and miter the corners for a neat finish (see inset).*

**5** *Using solder and a soldering iron, solder over the copper tape edge, following the manufacturer's instructions. The solder turns the copper silver, and makes the brooch waterproof and durable. Rub the soldered edges and the back of the brooch with steel wool dipped in a drop of dishwashing liquid and a tiny amount of water to tone down the shine. Dry thoroughly.*

**6** *To complete the brooch, apply Superglue on to a pin back, and position the pin back centrally and horizontally on the upper back of the brooch. Let the glue dry for at least an hour before wearing the brooch.*

# Painted Tin Brooch

**MATERIALS**

Paper
Sheet steel
Pin back
White matte
primer spray paint
Enamel paints

**EQUIPMENT**

Pen
Tin snips
Block of wood
Metal file
Wet-and-dry
sandpaper
Spot welder
Block of lead
Round-ended
hammer
Artist's brush

SHEET STEEL IS WONDERFULLY EASY to obtain. Making this brooch is a decorative way to recycle bean cans. A spot welder, on the other hand, is something that not everyone can get hold of or use with confidence. If this is your quandary, it is definitely worth experimenting with superglue for such a small project as this brooch.

Painted tin has a glossy slickness that makes it the perfect material for jokey, fun jewelry: you can paint any motif you like on it and you can make your brooch any shape, adding extra layers or fine detail as you wish, drawing inspiration from anything from comic books to medieval banners. If you are lucky enough to find tin cans printed with graphics or images that appeal to you, you can cut them out and use them as they are, or with witty additions of your own. Here, the designer has come up with a strong shape, which she has emphasized with bold primary colors. This is probably the most effective approach to humorous jewelry, but you might like to experiment with a subtle touch of verdigris or even rust. If you just don't feel dressed without a little sparkle, you could always wire a few beads or glue a few gems on to your creation. With junk jewelry, there is no excuse not to have fun.

**Star and Stripes**
*You may never get to be sheriff, but this badge is the perfect partner for a favorite faded denim shirt, and has its own real energy.*

**Steelworks**
*Enamel paints have an irresistible shine to them, and simply by changing the colors, and adding spots and stripes, you can create infinite variations on a theme of steel. Substituting a crescent moon for the heart varies the design even more.*

## Assembling the Brooch
*Cutting a hollow circle from steel is just about impossible, but by making it in three sections, you get the same effect with an interesting layered look.*

Sheet steel

Flat white primer spray paint

Pin back

Enamel paints

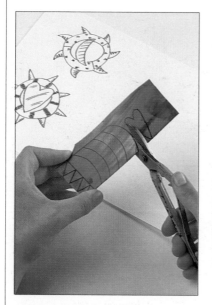

**1** Sketch the design for your brooch on a piece of paper. Then draw all the components of the design on to a piece of sheet steel. Carefully cut out all the pieces using tin snips.

**2** Taking each piece of steel in turn, place it on a block of wood, and holding it down, rub all the edges with a file to smooth. Then sand all the edges with wet-and-dry sandpaper.

**3** Using a spot welder, weld the three curved pieces of steel together to form a basic circular shape. Trim the edges with tin snips to neaten the circle.

4 Shape the metal heart and circle by holding them, one at a time, over a block of lead, then beating them lightly with a round-ended hammer. This gives the shapes a three-dimensional effect, making the brooch slightly convex in appearance when pinned on to clothing.

5 Weld the heart on to the basic circle at the three outermost points. Then weld on the five spikes around the edge of the circle. Turn the brooch over, and weld a pin back centrally and horizontally on to the upper back of the heart (see inset).

6 Working in a well-ventilated area, spray the metal brooch with a coat of flat white primer to create a good surface to paint on. Let the paint dry thoroughly. Using enamel paints, paint the heart red, the circle yellow, and the spikes blue. Allow the colors to merge together for a subtle effect.

7 Leave the first paint colors to dry, then paint thin blue stripes around the yellow circle for extra decoration. Let the brooch dry thoroughly before wearing it. There is no need to varnish the brooch, because the enamel paints provide a high-gloss coating and seal the metal against rust very effectively.

# Mixed–Media Brooch

## MATERIALS

Paper

Metallic silk

Colored silk

Machine embroidery threads

Sheet brass, ½₂in (0.7mm) thick

Balsa wood, ⅛in (2mm) thick

Water-based ink

Adhesive tape

Pin back

Wire, ⅟₁₆in (1mm) thick

Double-sided tape

4 brass circles

## EQUIPMENT

Pen

Pins

Embroidery hoop

Sewing machine and darning foot

Scissors

Block of wood

Clamp

Coping saw

Metal file

Hobby drill and ⅟₁₆in (1mm) drill bit

Sandpaper

Artist's brush

Wire cutters

Hammer

Anvil

IF YOU HAVE EVER PLAYED with a doll's house, you will know the fascination of miniature objects. This stitched brooch is, in effect, a tiny framed work of art; with nimble-fingered perseverance, you could aspire to a whole gallery for your lapel. But, to look good, tiny things require a meticulous finish - the smaller an object is, the more conspicuous are its defects to the inevitable close inspection. So, when you are making this embroidered brooch, go slowly and be careful with each stage, and the final result will be a fascinating and unique piece of art.

Machine embroidery is quick, easy, and can draw on the dazzling spectrum of colors to be found wherever needles and pins are sold. A Piscean pair of unknown species adorns this brooch, but you could use any simple, bold, and colorful motif — a summer strawberry, a Valentine heart, a starfish, your initials, a bluebird — that strikes you as being meaningful or pretty. There is no reason why you should not change the size or shape of your brooch, keeping in mind that straight edges are easier to cut with a coping saw, or embellish its diminutive frame with light-catching studs or tiny copper nail-heads. Instead of painting your wooden frame with colored ink, you might like to use a square of gold leaf or gold antiquing wax to enrich and decorate the frame.

### Fantastic Fish
*Bright primary colors and an arresting and appealing image combine to make the recipe for these stitched fish. The stitching gives a shiny relief texture to the fish and background, almost like scales and water.*

### Metal Petals
*Glowing satin-smooth stitches make the heart of these brooches. The brooches can pulsate with an entire rainbow of threads, or radiate calm with a trio of subtle and mutually flattering colors.*

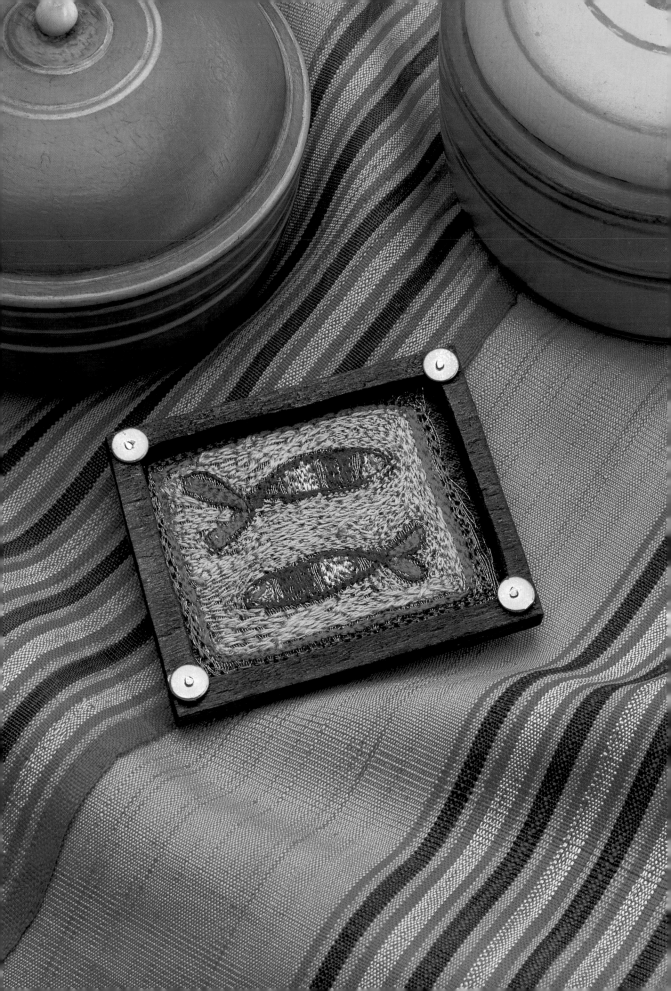

## Assembling the Brooch
*Making this brooch will require a little patience;*
*stitching and sawing may take practice. Still, you could always*
*cheat with the pin back and stick it on with glue.*

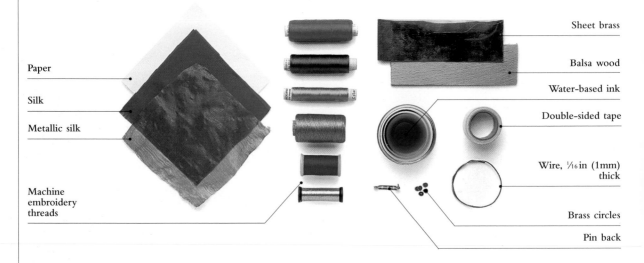

Paper

Silk

Metallic silk

Machine
embroidery
threads

Sheet brass

Balsa wood

Water-based ink

Double-sided tape

Wire, 1/16 in (1mm)
thick

Brass circles

Pin back

**1** *Sketch out the design for your brooch on a piece of paper. Here, the design is of a fish, but you could choose any motif you like, although simple, easily recognized motifs generally work better on this scale. Pin a small rectangle of metallic silk to a larger piece of silk. Put this in an embroidery hoop.*

**2** *Set the sewing machine for straight stitch, and thread it with machine embroidery thread. Keeping the feed dog down, and using the darning foot, stitch your brooch design on the silk rectangle. Fill in the design with stitching in different colors of thread so the entire design is filled with stitching. Cut out the rectangle, and set aside.*

**3** *Attach a block of wood to a work surface using a clamp. With one hand, hold a piece of sheet brass on the wood so the end protrudes over the edge of the wood. With the other hand, cut out a rectangle from the brass using a coping saw. The rectangle should be slightly larger than the embroidered silk rectangle. Smooth the rough edges with a file.*

**4** Using the coping saw, cut out a rectangle of wood the same size as the sheet brass. Drill a hole in the center of the wood with a small hobby drill. Insert the coping saw through the hole, and cut out the center of the wood to make a frame. Sand all rough edges with sandpaper.

**5** Using an artist's brush, paint the wooden frame on the front and back with a coat of water-based ink to stain it. Then set the frame aside to dry for at least 30 minutes.

**6** Tape the pin back to the upper center of the brass rectangle. Place the brass on to a block of wood; drill two holes in the pin back. Insert an ⅛in (2mm) length of wire into each hole. Hammer the wires on both sides of the brass; the ends will splay out to rivet the pin back to the brass.

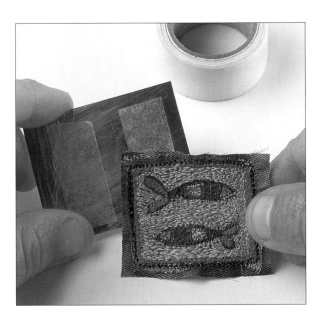

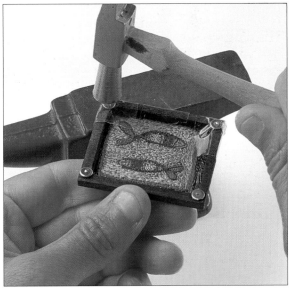

**7** Turn the brass rectangle over so the pin back is on the underside. Place two pieces of double-sided tape on to the brass. Trim any loose threads on the embroidered silk rectangle, then stick it down carefully on the brass, making sure that the edges of the embroidered silk do not protrude over the brass rectangle.

**8** Place the wooden frame over the embroidery and drill a hole through each corner. Tape a brass circle on each corner. Then, holding the brooch over an anvil, hammer an ⅛in (2mm) length of wire through each brass circle and through the layers of the brooch; the wire ends will splay out as you hammer them to rivet the layers together. Hammer the wire ends on the back of the brooch to secure.

# Etched Metal Earrings

## MATERIALS

Graph paper
Tracing paper
Sheet brass
Adhesive tape
Sheet steel
Printer's stop
(etching ground)
Turpentine
Nitric acid
Water
Pumice powder
Flux
Solder
Earring findings
Silver tubing, ⅛in
(2mm) thick

## EQUIPMENT

Pen
Scissors
Scriber
Block of wood
Coping saw
Metal files
Artist's brush
Rubber gloves
Apron
Goggles
Small lidded dish
Soft brush
Brass brush
Tweezers
Blow torch
Drill and ¹⁄₁₆in
(1mm) drill bit
Tin punch
Hammer
Glass brush
Soft cloth

THE STARTING POINT for these intricate earrings is to press your nose up against the glass in a museum of heraldry and armor. There you can search for the most regal shape of crest or shield to use as your basic outline. You could plagiarize the odd motif too, or you could simply reproduce the etched heraldic earrings shown here, which could hardly be bettered.

This is one of the more demanding projects in the book and could be described as professional jewelry. You will have to approach the project with caution, because some of the processes are tricky and potentially dangerous, but the raw materials are not costly and making the earrings will allow you to explore those rarefied realms beyond shiny baubles. Fortunately, symmetry is optional; if both earrings do not match exactly, that is part of the charm of making your own jewelry. Anyone can buy machine-made bijoux, perfect and matching but lacking soul or character. These earrings, however, evoke the distant echoes of bugle fanfares, royal banners, and legendary monarchs, and are all the better for their individual quirks. You could, to start with, fashion a simplified shape based on a shield, and work up to elaborate coronet shapes. After you have made a pair of earrings, a brooch will be child's play.

**Heraldic Devices**
*Of course, no one would dream of wearing another person's coat of arms, but there is nothing to stop you from experimenting with some of the bold charges, devices, and blazoning of medieval heraldry.*

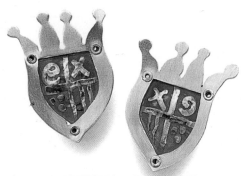

**Copper and Steel**
*The same earrings, but this time made from sheet steel and copper, have a subtler and more discreet effect. Try combining different metals, such as gold and silver, for total glamour.*

## Making the Earrings

*Making these earrings requires dexterity, as well as
a cool head with nitric acid and a blowtorch. However,
success is really something to be proud of.*

Silver tubing

Graph paper

Sheet steel

Sheet brass

Earring findings

Printer's stop

Nitric acid

Soldering flux

Pumice powder

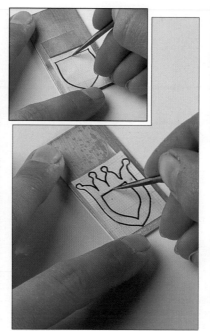

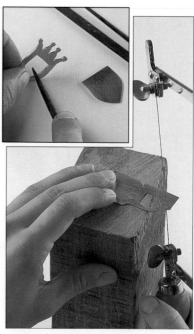

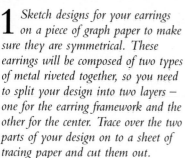

**1** *Sketch designs for your earrings on a piece of graph paper to make sure they are symmetrical. These earrings will be composed of two types of metal riveted together, so you need to split your design into two layers – one for the earring framework and the other for the center. Trace over the two parts of your design on to a sheet of tracing paper and cut them out.*

**2** *To make one earring, tape the tracing for the framework of the design on to a piece of sheet brass with adhesive tape. Using a scriber, score over the design lines on the tracing. This will transfer the design to the metal beneath. Then tape the tracing for the center of the design over a piece of sheet steel, and repeat the scoring with that design (see inset).*

**3** *Holding the scored brass and steel, one at a time, on a block of wood, saw along the scored lines of the earring design with a coping saw to cut out the two parts of the earring. File all the edges of both pieces with a metal file, using a small file for more intricately-shaped corners (see inset).*

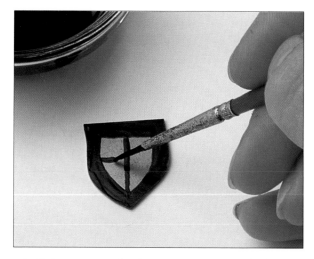

**4** Using an artist's brush, paint printer's stop (etching ground) on the back of the steel, around the edges, and on the front in a simple design. (The printer's stop should be runny; if it feels too thick, you can thin it down with a little turpentine.) The metal that is covered with the printer's stop will not be etched out in the next step. Let the steel piece dry for approximately 30 minutes.

**5** Work in a well-ventilated area to avoid inhaling toxic fumes, and wear rubber gloves, apron, and goggles. Add 1 part nitric acid to 5 parts water in a bowl and mix well. Put the steel in the bowl and cover. When bubbles appear on the steel, brush them away gently with a soft brush. Cover, and let the steel stand; repeat the brushing every 10 minutes. In 30 minutes the acid will etch out the metal that has not been covered with printer's stop.

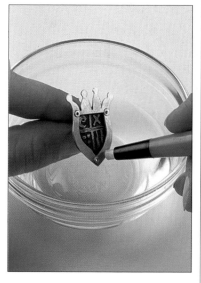

**6** Remove the steel from the bowl, rinse in cold water, and brush off the printer's stop using a brass brush dipped in pumice powder and water. To attach the earring finding to the back of the steel, apply flux and solder to the metal. Using tweezers, hold the earring finding in position on the solder and heat the solder with a blowtorch to fuse the finding in place.

**7** Place the steel piece of the earring behind the brass piece and rivet the two together. To do this, drill a hole in each of the three corners. Insert an ⅛in (2mm) length of silver tubing into each drilled hole, insert a tin punch into the tubing to open up the end, and hammer the tin punch to flatten the tubing to secure. Repeat on both sides of the earring.

**8** Clean the earring for maximum shine using a glass brush and water. Then, wipe it with a soft cloth for a final polish. Repeat steps 2 to 8 to make a matching earring. When you have completed the earrings, clean all brushes with turpentine.

# Ideas to Inspire

Wood and metal are both reassuringly solid materials with character and attraction. There is plenty of inspiration here to satisfy the most discerning eye, and plenty to keep occupied the most adept hand. There is ingenuity enough to reveal marvels where before you had only junk. A trip to your local hardware store – all those shiny chains, washers, wires, and assorted metal – will make you faint with excitement. So start welding!

▼ **Chain Reaction**
*These delicate steel wire rectangles were easily formed and looped together with pliers to make a necklace. A cutout silver pendant, based on ancient Indian architecture, hangs from one of the links.*

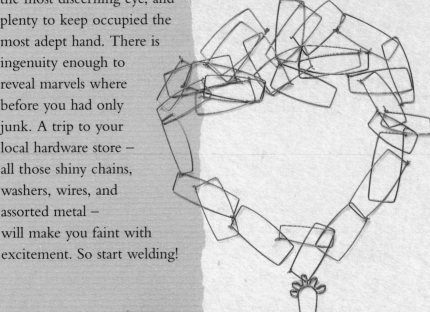

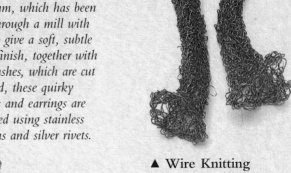

► **Miniature Gallery**
*These tiny works of art are executed on sheet copper using a variety of paint techniques to create textural, metallic patterns. The pieces are then covered with picture-framing glass and framed with copper tape, which is soldered to give a silvery finish. A pin back is glued onto the back.*

◄ **Dental Adornment**
*Made from anodized aluminum, which has been rolled through a mill with paper to give a soft, subtle surface finish, together with toothbrushes, which are cut and filed, these quirky brooches and earrings are assembled using stainless steel pins and silver rivets.*

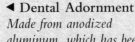

▲ **Wire Knitting**
*Copper-colored wire and shimmering purple yarn are knitted together to create these horn-shaped earrings, using four needles to give hollow centers.*

▶ **Riveting Silk**

*Tiny snippets of machine-embroidered silk are here sandwiched between sheet brass and picture-framing glass, and held in position with brass rivets or screws in each corner. Pin backs are riveted to the backs.*

▶ **Fishy Finery**

*These inventive brooches are made entirely from recycled materials. The two large fish are made from sheet steel, which is etched with wax and sulfuric acid; the baby fish are made from plastic and enameled steel, then attached with laminated mesh.*

◀ **Beaded Hat Pins**

*Simple, yet stylish, these hat pins are decorated with a combination of colored and silver beads, which are glued in place with superglue.*

### ◀ Baroque Pins
*Intricate machine-embroidery, backed by sunbursts of sheet brass and embellished with golden curlicues and beads, decorates this duo of resplendent hat pins.*

### ▼ Welded Steel
*These pewterish brooches are made from pieces of sheet steel welded together, then given light-catching texture using a hammer and center punch.*

### ▼ Live Wire
*Colored glass and plastic beads are threaded onto copper wire, then wrapped around with more wire to create bangles and a necklace. Silver stars are secured to the necklace using strong thread.*

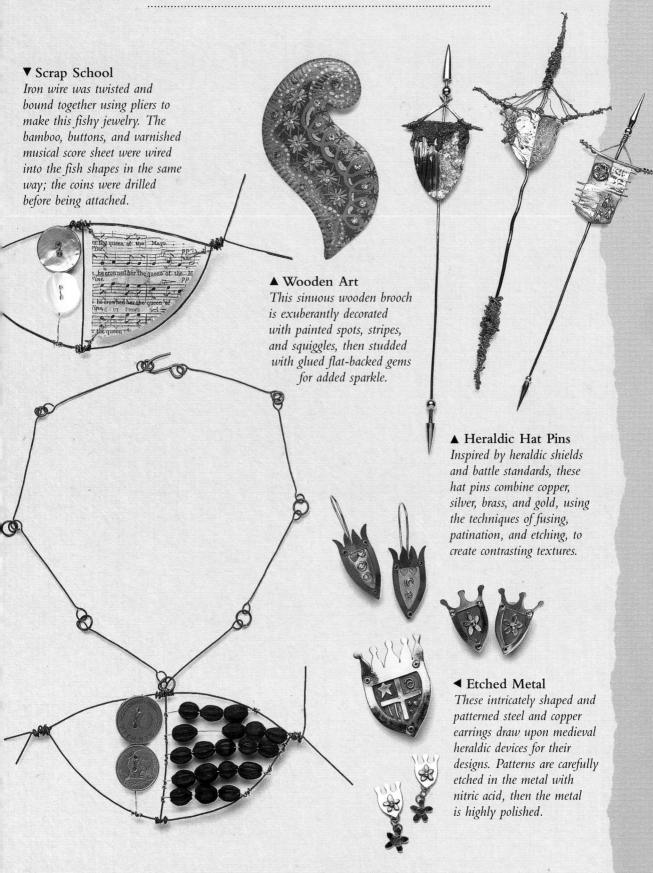

▼ **Scrap School**

*Iron wire was twisted and bound together using pliers to make this fishy jewelry. The bamboo, buttons, and varnished musical score sheet were wired into the fish shapes in the same way; the coins were drilled before being attached.*

▲ **Wooden Art**

*This sinuous wooden brooch is exuberantly decorated with painted spots, stripes, and squiggles, then studded with glued flat-backed gems for added sparkle.*

▲ **Heraldic Hat Pins**

*Inspired by heraldic shields and battle standards, these hat pins combine copper, silver, brass, and gold, using the techniques of fusing, patination, and etching, to create contrasting textures.*

◀ **Etched Metal**

*These intricately shaped and patterned steel and copper earrings draw upon medieval heraldic devices for their designs. Patterns are carefully etched in the metal with nitric acid, then the metal is highly polished.*

# Contributors

**The Author**
*pp.70-71 top*

**Deborah Alexander**
*pp.52-55*
Tel: 01403 241563
14 Barrington Road, Horsham
West Sussex RH13 5SN

**Julie Arkell**
*pp.38-41; p.48 bottom right;*
*p.49 top left*
Tel: 0171-916 6447
Unit W8, Cockpit Workshops
Cockpit Yard
Northington Street
London WC1N 2NP

**Louise Baldwin**
*pp.26-29*
Tel: 0171-639 2765
18 Reynolds Road
London SE15 3AH

**Victoria Brown**
*pp.30-33; p.47 bottom right*
Tel: 0171-708 5559
88 Lyndhurst Grove
London SE15 5AH

**Jane Burns**
*p.91 bottom left*
Tel: 0171-607 8043
265B Liverpool Road
London N1 1LX

**Sheila Churchill/**
**Jacqueline Roberts**
*p.70 left*
Tel: 0181-994 4297
The Wild Jewellery Company
2 Mulberry House
Cavendish Road
London W4 3UH

**Judy Clayton**
*pp.42-45; p.92 top left*
Tel: 01273 603437
Flat 3
16 Lower Rock Gardens
Brighton
East Sussex BN2 1PG

**Sally Cochrane**
*pp.82-85; p.91 top right*
Tel: 01273 725321
14 Cross Street
Hove, East Sussex

**Philippa Crawford**
*pp.74-77; pp.90-91 top*
Tel: 0131-557 0109
26 Drummond Place
Edinburgh
Lothian EH3 6PN

**Sarah Crawford**
*p.90 bottom left*
Tel: 0181-340 6829
104B Hillfield Avenue
Crouch End
London N8 7DN

**Alison Dane**
*p.47 top right; p.48 bottom right*
Tel: 01359 258852
Crownlands Cottage
Walsham-le-Willows
Suffolk IP31 3BU

**Lill Gardner**
*p.69 top right*
Tel: 0171-372 2502
22 Buckley Road
Brondesbury
London NW6 7NA

**Janice Gilmore**
*pp.34-37; p.49 right*
Tel: 01232 654867
28 Cyprus Park, Belfast
Northern Ireland BT5 6EA

**Ray Halsall**
*pp.64-67; p.68 bottom left;*
*p.69 bottom right*
Tel: 0171-272 5164
14B Cressida Road
Archway, London N19 3JW

**Deidre Hawken**
*p.46 top*
Tel: 0181-858 7091
35 Glenluce Road
Blackheath, London SE3 7SD

**Tracy Hazlett**
*p.48 top left; p.90 top left*
*and bottom right*
Tel: 01506 871235
16 Gloag Place, West Calder
West Lothian EH55 8DW

**Gwen Hedley**
*pp.18-21*
Tel: 01494 873850
Oronsay, Misbourne Avenue
Chalfont St Peter
Buckinghamshire SL9 0PF

**Julie Howells**
*p.48 center*
Tel: 01344 773866
35 Greenwood Road
Crowthorne
Berkshire RG45 6JS

**Lesley Anne Hutchings**
*pp.68-69 bottom*
Tel: 01273 774393
62a Goldstone Road
Hove, East Sussex BN3 3RH

**Judy Ironside**
*pp.14-17*
Tel: 01273 540642
35 Claremont Terrace
Preston Park, Brighton
East Sussex BN1 6SJ

**Helyne Jennings**
*p.49 bottom left*
Tel: 01769 520633
Pennyford Cottage
Burrington, Umberleigh
Devon EX37 9LN

**Thérèse Kane**
*p.93 top right*
Tel: 01788 536352
11 Fellows Way
Hillmorton, Rugby
Warwickshire CV21 4JP

**Diana Laurie**
*pp.68-69 top; p.69 center;*
*p.92 bottom right*
Tel: 0171-831 6212
Unit 5, Cockpit Workshops
Cockpit Yard
Northington Street
London WC1N 2NP

**Rachel Lucas/Ella Jennings**
*p.47 bottom left*
Tel: 0171-624 6812
Flat 2, 43 Aberdare Gardens
South Hampstead
London NW6 3AL

**Rachel Maidens**
*p.70 bottom*
Tel: 01909 564408
51 Devonshire Drive
North Anston, Nr Sheffield
South Yorkshire S31 7AN

**Louise Nelson**
*p.47 top left*
Tel: 01292 671626
9 Hillside Crescent
Prestwick, Ayrshire KA9 2JN

**Polly Plouviez**
*pp.56-59*
Tel: 0171-916 0155
Unit W5, Cockpit Workshops
Cockpit Yard
Northington Street
London WC1N 2NP

**Anna Pritchard**
*pp.86-89; p.93 bottom left*
Tel: 0171-242 0519
Unit 4, Cockpit Workshops
Cockpit Yard
Northington Street
London WC1N 2NP

**Lizzie Reakes**
*pp.22-25; p46 bottom left*
Tel: 0181-840 7579
68 Oaklands Road
Hanwell, Ealing
London W7 2DU

**John Shortall**
*p.71 right*
26 Cooper Close
London SE1 7QU

**Claire Sowden**
*p.48 top right*
Tel: 01252 870334
6 Bramling Avenue
Yateley, Camberley
Surrey GU17 7NX

**Alison Start**
*pp.78-81; p.92 bottom left*
Tel: 01273 674809
12 Arnold Street
Brighton
East Sussex BN2 2XT

**Sam Vettese**
*pp.92-93 top; p.93 bottom left*
Tel: 01506 880917
Almond House
Mid Calder
EH53 0AX

**Sara Withers**
*pp.60-63*
Tel: 01865 862197
Old Cottage
Appleton, Abingdon
Oxfordshire OX13 5JH

# Index

# Acknowledgments

The most enormous thanks are due to the designers and jewelers who have dreamed up, refined, and perfected the sumptuous and sassy objects in these pages. The mark of a true creative spirit is an extraordinary generosity; every one of the artists and craftspeople who contributed to this book was happy to share hard-won secrets and techniques with the world, probably because genuine innovators are always generating new ideas and moving on. Those of us who are not such creative powerhouses are in the happy position of being able to applaud and learn. In addition, the dedicated team who put this book together could not possibly be bettered: Clive Streeter took all the photographs with his usual perceptiveness and intelligence, and was an endless fount of good cheer and great ideas. He was efficiently helped out by Andy Whitfield, who also kept us fed and full of caffeine. Marnie Searchwell designed the book and was tirelessly perfectionist in her pursuit of faultless composition. Ali Edney sped around London in search of the essential props to show off the jewelry. That the whole unwieldy operation came together so brilliantly is entirely thanks to Heather Dewhurst, who documented every step with minute accuracy, and made it all comprehensible. Besides resulting in a handsome book, working with such a bunch of people is good for the soul and the giggle muscles.

*The following companies kindly loaned props for photography:*

**The Bead Shop**
43 Neal Street
Covent Garden
London WC2H 9JP
Tel: 0171-240 0831
*Fastenings and tools*

**Cowling & Wilcox Limited**
26-28 Broadwick Street
London W1V 1FG
Tel: 0171-734 5781
*Artist's materials*

**Fired Earth Tiles plc**
21 Battersea Square
London SW11 3RA
Tel: 0171-924 2272
*Slate tile on p.53*

**Liberty**
Regent Street
London W1R 6AH
Tel: 0171-734 1234
*Black wool jacket on p.31; wooden box on p.61; red wool crêpe jacket on p.65*

**Spread Eagle Antiques**
8 Nevada Street
London SE10 9LJ
Tel: 0181-305 1666
*Silver chain mail purse on p.87*